Foreword

**By Maria Welch,
Head of Magazines, DC Thomson**

I WAS extremely fortunate to hold various posts on "Jackie" magazine, including deputy editor. It was hands-down the best job I have ever had, where happy memories and lifelong friends were made.

The "Jackie" team grew up together and grew up with our readers. "Jackie" was the emotional support system for a generation of teenage girls, and that's why it still holds a special place in hearts decades later. It seems inconceivable now that the biggest celebrities of the day would make their way to the north-east coast of Scotland to the "Jackie" office within the amazing DC Thomson building in the centre of Dundee.

It was also common for us to use the historic graveyard across the road for moody photoshoots – Adam Ant leaning on a gravestone on a miserable November day turned out to be a best-selling cover shot!

Fortunately for "Jackie" readers and, more importantly, the "Jackie" team, our minor indiscretions committed due to the exuberance of youth went largely unnoticed. If you were really unlucky, they went around the third floor of Thomson Towers, but they certainly didn't go around the world on social media.

So, let us take you back to the days when there was no Botox or Brazilian butt-lifts, and where most problems in life could be solved with a spray of Batiste Dry Shampoo and a slick of Rimmel's Heather Shimmer lippie – please note other brands are available but they just won't look as good!

Once a "Jackie" girl – ALWAYS a "Jackie" girl!

Maria

Contents

P6 – "Jackie", The Ultimate 'It' Girl

P8 – COVER STORY
Iconic front pages from "Jackie's" heyday

P16 – MUSIC MATTERS
Why pop was at the heart of "Jackie"
P18 – Superstars of the 60s
P26 – Icons of the 70s
P34 – Sounds of the 80s
P42 – The Ultimate 80s Pop Quiz!

P46 – FASHION AND BEAUTY
Decades of magical style advice
P48 – Perfect hair whatever the occasion!
P50 – The beauty box
P52 – Pinny-Wise!
P54 – Make A Contrast
P56 – Win His Heart!
P57 – Shape Up To The 80s!
P58 – Juicy Fruits!
P60 – Party Party!
P62 – Layer It On!
P64 – Look Out
P66 – Be His Heart-Throb!
P68 – Get the 80s look
P70 – Seeing Stars – Lesley Ash
P72 – Famous Faces
P74 – Top Pop Trio
P76 – Super Sadie
P78 – Spotted!
P80 – Style Queens

P82 – MATTERS OF THE HEART
Or, in other words – boys!
P84 – Photo story: Between The Lines
P87 – Photo story: Happy Families
P90 – Photo story: Wishing I Was Lucky
P93 – Photo story: Horsing Around!
P98 – How Romantic Are You? Fun quiz
P101 – Love Letters
P102 – What's He Hiding?
P104 – Your "Jackie" Guide To . . . Kissing!
P106 – What's In Store For You In 1981?

P108 – WORD TO THE WISE
Why "Jackie" had all the answers
P110 – Cathy & Claire
P112 – Dear Ellie

P114 – MAGICAL MEMORIES
Behind the scenes at "Jackie"
P116 – "I was a 'Jackie' cover star"
P118 – Work It Out!
P120 – Staff memories – Wendy Rigg
P122 – Staff memories – Jackie Brown
P123 – Secrets of life at "Jackie"
P124 – Staff memories – Fiona Gibson
P126 – Staff memories – Tracey Steel, Gayle Anderson and Mike Soutar
P128 – Staff memories – Lucy Crichton

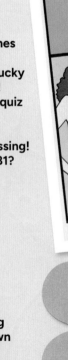

p52 PI

p38

p21

p56

p11

p42

p110

CREDITS

Editor: Stuart Johnstone
Design Editor: Wendy Dempster-Corlett
Content Editor: Tracey Steel
Illustrator: Manon Gandiolle
With thanks to: Sue Dando and Graeme Strachan
Special Thanks to the DC Thomson Archive Team –
Barry Sullivan   Melissa Lonie
Gary Thomas   Niamh Quinn

Images: DCT Archive and Shutterstock unless otherwise stated.

Published in the UK by DC Thomson & Co Ltd, Dundee, Glasgow and London. © DC Thomson & Co Ltd, 2024. Registered Office: DC Thomson & Co Ltd, Courier Buildings, 2 Albert Square, Dundee, Scotland, DD1 9QJ. Distributed by Frontline Ltd, Stuart House, St John's St, Peterborough, Cambridgeshire PE1 5DD. Tel: +44 (0) 1733 555161. Website: www.frontlinedistribution.co.uk. Export distribution (excluding AU and NZ) Seymour Distribution Ltd, 2 East Poultry Avenue, London EC1A 9PT. Tel: +44(0)20 7429 4000. Fax: +44(0)20 7429 4001. Website: www.seymour.co.uk. EU Representative Office: DC Thomson & Co Ltd, c/o Findmypast Ireland, Irishtown, Athlone, Co. Westmeath, N37 XP52. Editorial communications to "Jackie - 60 Years Of Magic", 2 Albert Square, Dundee DD1 1DD. While every reasonable care will be taken, neither D.C. Thomson & Co., Ltd., nor its agents will accept liability for loss or damage to any materials submitted to this publication. Jackie - 60 Years of Magic is a member of IPSO (the Independent Press Standards Organisation), which regulates the UK's newspaper, magazine, and digital news industry. We abide by the Editors' Code of Practice and are committed to upholding the highest standards of journalism. If you think that we have not met those standards and want to make a complaint, please contact readerseditor@dcthomson.co.uk or Readers Editor, Jackie - 60 Years Of Magic, DC Thomson & Co Ltd, Courier Buildings, 2 Albert Square, Dundee, Scotland, DD1 9QJ. If we are unable to resolve your complaint, or if you would like more information about IPSO or the Editors' Code, contact IPSO on 0300 123 2220 or visit www.ipso.co.uk

IPSO Regulated   DC THOMSON

Jackie
The Ultimate "It" Girl

I N a flurry of glitz, glamour and glitter, "Jackie" was launched 60 years ago, on January 11 1964. "Top Of The Pops" had just aired on BBC 1 for the first time and The Beatles were moving swiftly towards the peak of their fame. "Jackie" was born as the Swinging Sixties really began to take off!

Packed with beauty tips, picture strip stories, fashion, colour pop pin-ups and heartfelt advice, "Jackie" was a girl's best friend, as well as being the magazine to be seen with.

"Jackie" was created, printed and published by DC Thomson in Dundee. To test the water in the teen market for "Jackie", a one-off pop title was produced.

The 64-page magazine was called "Elvis, Cliff and All".

It was put together by a small team and included "pop, pin-ups, stories and features" about stars of the day, including Elvis Presley, Cliff Richard, Adam Faith and Billy Fury.

A double page was devoted to the loves of Elvis Presley's life, and glossy posters included actors Warren Beatty, Richard Chamberlain and Clint Eastwood.

And, if you were creative, you could construct the "perfect boy" from cut-out hairstyles, eyes, noses and lips belonging to Roy Castle, Jess Conrad, Adam Faith, Shane Fenton and Cliff Richard.

Only a small number were printed and placed with selected newsagents, but it was a big hit!

Amazingly, the most famous girls' mag of all time almost wasn't called "Jackie" .

President John F Kennedy was assassinated in November 1963, just after the first edition of "Jackie" had gone to press – 12 weeks before publication date – and there were concerns about the publication bearing his widow's name. However, it was decided to go ahead with the initial print run of around 500,000.

The cover of the first issue featured Cliff Richard with a giveaway of a free twin heart ring.

It was headed "Jackie For Go-Ahead Teens" and sold 350,000 copies.

Its founder was a former RAF aero engine fitter called Gordon Small who, with his love for hillwalking and motorbiking, was an unlikely person to be at the helm of a teenage girls' magazine.

What the staff did have in common was enormous enthusiasm for the product. They loved it, and that shone through on every page.

Teenage girls loved it just as much. They lined up to pay the 6d (2.5p) to find out what was happening in the world, to keep up with all the gossip and advice on the all-important matters of boys and beauty!

Today's teenagers may be much more savvy but, for "Jackie"

60s

February 1, 1964. Every Thursday 6d

Jackie
for go-ahead teens

FREE THE 1964 HAIRSTYLE BOOK

FULL-COLOUR PIN-UPS—
VINCE EDWARDS, EDEN
KANE, RINGO AND THIS
ONE OF ELVIS!

FRILLY, FLOUNCY, FEMININE
—the very latest in slinky
sleepwear on pages 18 and
19. All in colour!

BE A BEAUTY COVER-UPPER—
TOP-MODEL SECRETS ON PAGE 6

CLIFF ON HOLIDAY IN
SPAIN—2 pages of
many colour pictures!

BRIAN HYLAND PIX, YOUR
HOROSCOPE, PETE LENNON'S
POP GOSSIP, ANOTHER NEW
HAIRSTYLE! MORE! MORE!

Jackie HAS EVERYTHING!

70s

No. 503 AUGUST 25th, 1973 THURSDAYS 4p

Jackie

FOCUS, ALICE & NEW SEEKERS PIN-UPS THIS WEEK!

devotees, there was only one trusted source to turn to for help – the Cathy and Claire problem pages.

By the 1970s the warm wisdom and insight saw sackfuls of letters arriving in the offices every week.

Of course, Cathy and Claire weren't real and over the years several people took on the mantle.

The letters were initially sent to the Fleet Street office in London then made their way in overnight lorries to the magazine's home in Dundee.

With the sometimes overwhelming feelings the teenage years can bring, it was a combination of big sister and best friend – a kind voice in a world that was often perceived to be cruel.

As The Beatles broke up and the 60s gave way to the 70s, "Jackie" magazine's popularity soared.

The issue with a free poster of David Cassidy sold an incredible 1.1 million copies on October 21, 1972.

It was the halcyon days for print.

In every girl's room in the 1970s, the posters of Donny Osmond, David Cassidy, Slade and the Bay City Rollers would have been there courtesy of "Jackie" magazine.

Some of the most-loved posters came in three parts, with the head and shoulders kept until last.

These wonderful creative flourishes meant that, even as many competitor titles came and went, "Jackie" remained the number one choice for its readers.

It helped that most of the staff on "Jackie" were barely above the age of the readers.

These included famous names like BBC broadcaster Jackie Bird, who worked in the Dundee office in the

1970s and became Jackie from "Jackie" with a weekly "Jackie Goes Into Action" page in the magazine.

"Antiques Roadshow" presenter Fiona Bruce was a "Jackie" photo model from 1980, while Hollywood actor Alan Cumming appeared in the 1984 photo story "Horsing Around".

Over the decades, "Jackie" moved with the times, but it never changed from producing features from the heart, giving the young audience exactly what it wanted.

That warm, always positive and enthusiastic approach existed right up to the last issue, which hit the shelves in 1993.

However, although the magazine is no longer produced, the spirit of "Jackie" lives on.

Once a "Jackie" girl, always a "Jackie" girl.

80s

No. 958 MAY 15, 1982 THURSDAYS 16p (IR 24p inc. VAT)

Jackie

...Wilde and Wonderful!

EXCLUSIVE! KIM WILDE talks about fashion

COVER Story

IMAGINE the excitement: it's Thursday morning. You wake up, leap out of bed, check your pocket money jar on the table and get ready for the day.

Top priority? Dashing to the newsagent to see which star was on the cover of the latest issue of "Jackie" magazine.

You arrive at the newsstand, allowing your eyes to fall upon the many, many titles that line the shelves, each vying to stand out from the crowd.

"Jackie" was one title where the cover always made an impact.

The covers are works of art, as well as being a story of the time.

Looking back at those all-important front pages is like taking a walk through recent history.

Want to know who was topping the charts in early 1971? Look at "Jackie" from that era.

Want to know what fashion and beauty trends girls were obsessing about in the late 1980s? Look at "Jackie" from that era.

Lovingly compiled by a dedicated team of artists and editors, the "Jackie" covers were a shop window to the content inside.

It became the highlight of the week for many young readers – scanning the coverlines to see what goss they were going to read, what advice they were going to learn, and what eye candy they would be putting up on their bedroom walls!

Over the next few pages we have compiled some of the most memorable covers. Is your favourite there?

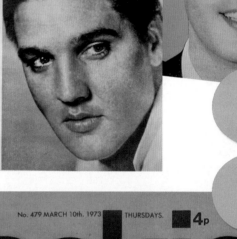

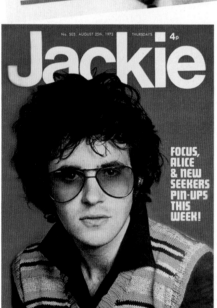

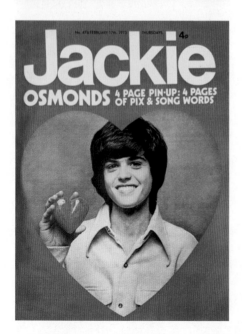

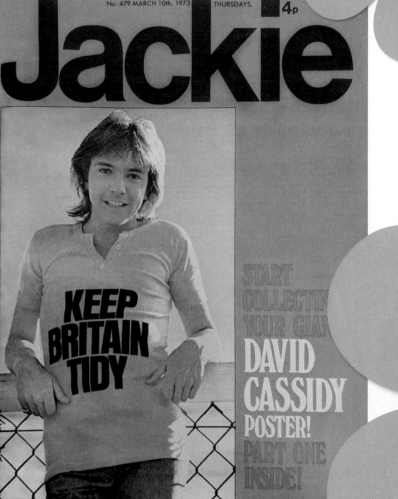

FREE POSTER INSIDE

No. 448 AUGUST 5th. 1972   THURSDAYS.   3½p

Jackie

GET YOUR HUGE FREE MARC POSTER INSIDE

FUN FACT: The biggest uplift in sales of "Jackie" magazine, to the tune of 243,000 extra units in just one week, was this August 5, 1972 issue featuring a huge Marc Bolan poster.

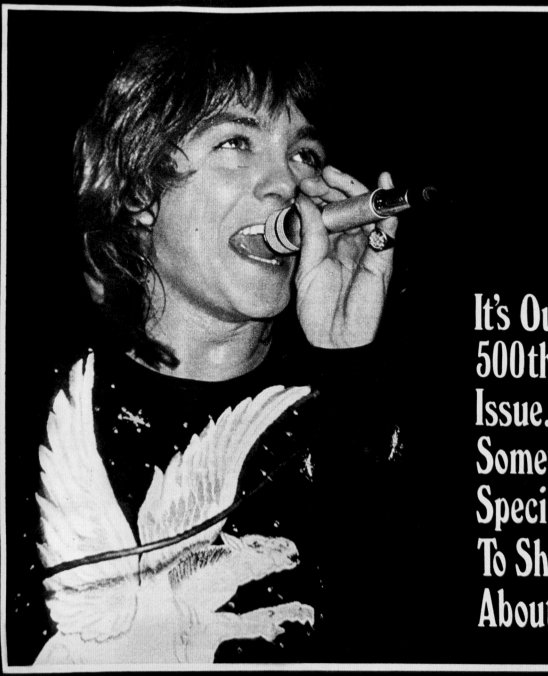

All Your Favourites... On One Super~Size Pop Pin~Up!

No 500 AUG 4th 1973   THURSDAYS   4p

Jackie

It's Our 500th Issue... Something Special To Shout About!

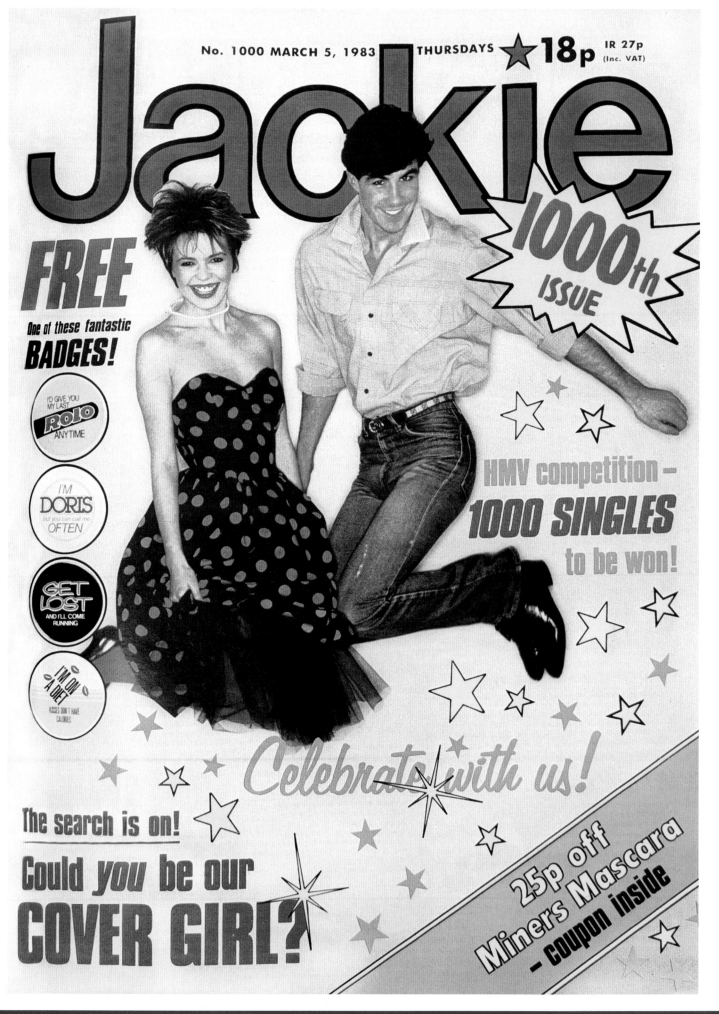

No. 1000 MARCH 5, 1983 THURSDAYS ★18p IR 27p (Inc. VAT)

Jackie

1000th ISSUE

FREE

One of these fantastic
BADGES!

I'D GIVE YOU MY LAST **Rolo** ANYTIME

I'M **DORIS** But you can call me OFTEN

GET LOST AND I'LL COME RUNNING

I'M ON A DIET KISSES DON'T HAVE CALORIES

HMV competition –
1000 SINGLES
to be won!

Celebrate with us!

The search is on!

Could *you* be our
COVER GIRL?

25p off
Miners Mascara
– coupon inside

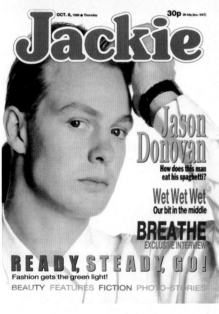

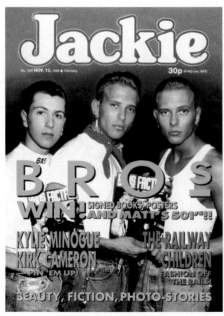

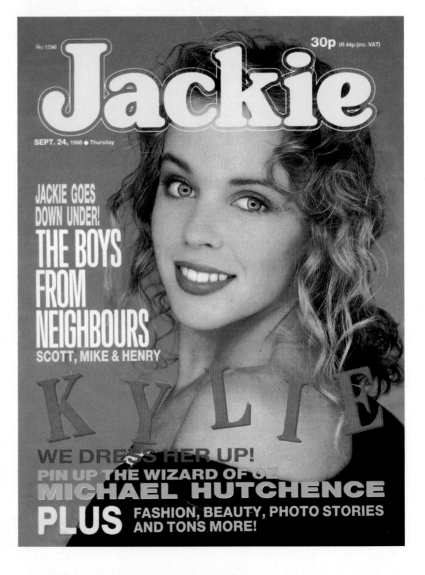

50p ★

JACKIE
MAGAZINE

NO. 1539 JULY 3, 1993
THURSDAY

LAST ISSUE EVER!

30 YEARS of JACKIE
From the 60s to the 90s
— we look back

Take THAT Past&Present
(we've got the pictures)...

9 770262 028036

PITT STOP 'Bye, Brad — you're the best! ▶▶▶

Music

AS the saying goes, music brings us together, and that was certainly the case for "Jackie" girls, who would gather round the magazine in bedrooms and living rooms across the land to catch up on the gossip about their favourite pop stars.

Over the decades, "Jackie" was the place to go to find out what was hip and happening in the chart world.

Icons such as David Cassidy, Donny Osmond, The Beatles, Marc Bolan and many more would regularly grace the covers.

"Jackie" was a window into a glamorous world that would inevitably feel exotic and exclusive to generations of adoring teenage fans.

The magazine would interview all the big names, getting all the info the young readers wanted to know.

Posters were carefully removed from the spine and would inevitably end up plastering walls across the nation.

Everyone had their favourite and over the next few pages, we will look back at some of the legendary singers, performers and indeed covers, that were so popular over the decades.

Jackie

Music

60s

The biggest names in pop music appeared in "Jackie". Here we look back at some of the 60s, 70s and 80s stars who graced the pages.

CLIFF RICHARD

Cliff Richard

Cliff Richard, who in his early career was marketed as Britain's answer to Elvis Presley, was a "Jackie" fan favourite. It was his face that shone out from the magazine's first ever cover in 1964. From the big quiff atop his head, Elvis-style clothes and rockstar poses, he was a worthy successor to the King and had multiple hit records and a successful TV and film career. Harry Webb's boyish good looks won the hearts of many a teenage girl in the 1960s and beyond. Between 1959 and 1963 he amassed 19 consecutive top four singles, including "Living Doll" and "The Young Ones", the title track from the hugely popular film of the same name. He even represented Britain twice in the Eurovision Song Contest with "Congratulations" and "Power To All Our Friends". Selling over 250 million records worldwide, many will fondly place his "Living Doll" Comic Relief performance with "The Young Ones" as a highlight.

The Beatles

It could be argued that the mop-headed quartet from Liverpool were the original boy band, such was their popularity with young fans in the 60s. Certainly, the hysteria they caused wherever they went was on a par with anything seen today, even if their music had more of a rock rather than pure pop feel to it. Formed in 1960, the Fab Four are still regarded as the most influential band in shaping pop culture as we know it, having a string of worldwide hits, most notably "Let It Be", "Hey Jude" and "She Loves You". Led by prolific songwriters Paul McCartney and John Lennon, they were bigger than anything before and certainly bigger than anything that followed them. The Beatles were the complete package: stylish; proficient musicians, with an undeniable knack for writing catchy tunes and, of course, they were very easy on the eye (it helped).

Elvis Presley

Elvis Presley was already a worldwide sensation when "Jackie" launched in 1964, so much so that he was one of the first stars to appear on the cover. It wasn't just the iconic vocals that got everyone's attention – he was quite simply gorgeous to look at. With his huge quiff and soulful eyes, the man who became known as the king of rock 'n' roll caused hoards of teenage girls to faint wherever he went and earned him the all-together racier nickname of Elvis the Pelvis due to the wild hip gyrations that accompanied his guitar playing. Detractors described his movements as "obscene", which instantly made him even more desirable to his fans. With a catalogue of hits including "Love Me Tender" and "Don't Be Cruel", and a raft of monstrously successful films to boot, Elvis forever changed the music industry and led a teenage revolution away from 1950s saccharine safety to an altogether more rebellious era.

Iconic Moment
The Swinging Sixties

The Swinging Sixties wasn't so much a moment – more of a seismic shift away from a post-war Britain getting back on its feet to a decade full of hope, adventure and freedom. It was a defining time for Britain, led by a youth culture that celebrated outrageous fashion (those Mary Quant miniskirts!), wild make-up (Twiggy's eyeliner!) and full-on hedonism (OMG – Woodstock!) It was an era led by music: the Beatles, the Rolling Stones and the Who were all part of what was known in the US as the "British Invasion". Pirate radio stations like Radio Caroline sprang up and London's Carnaby Street became the UK's fashion hub. It became known as the decade that shook Britain, and for good reason, as our little island became the centre of the world in terms of music and fashion – a label that still holds strong today.

Sandie Shaw

Bare-footed Dagenham girl Sandie Shaw had her first number one at the age of 17 and went on to claim a mass of chart toppers in the UK and a legion of female fans who aspired to be a cool as she was. Discovered in 1964 by singer Adam Faith, the sometime fashion model released "Always Something There To Remind Me" in 1964, and saw it soar to the top of the hit parade. In some ways she epitomised the Swinging Sixties era – miniskirts, the classic bob haircut and oversized floppy sun hats making up a large part of her look that was copied by teen girls up and down the country. At the height of her career, she won the Eurovision Song Contest with one of her biggest hits, the bouncy "Puppet On A String", a global number one that sealed her fate as one of the top female stars of the decade.

Petula Clark

Although she began performing on the radio as a child entertainer in concert and on BBC Radio during World War II, it was in the mid 1960s that Petula Clark's star began to truly shine. She recorded the classic song "Downtown" in 1964, which, although it was kept off the top of the charts by the Beatles in the UK, became a worldwide hit and catapulted her to international stardom. As an all-round entertainer she went on to star in two Hollywood musicals, "Finian's Rainbow" and "Goodbye Mr Chips" and became a regular guest on American variety shows hosted by luminaries Dean Martin and Harry Belafonte. She even trod the boards on stage starring as Maria Von Trapp in "The Sound of Music" and "Sunset Boulevard". Tellingly, she was the only person to be celebrated on TV show "This Is Your Life" three times.

The Jackson Five

Comprising five brothers – Jackie, Tito, Jermaine, Marlon and Michael Jackson – the Jackson Five rose to fame in the late 1960s and early 1970s with their catchy blend of pop, soul and R&B. Put together by their strict father, the band began performing in local talent shows and clubs, with young Michael, at the time only six, quickly emerging as the charismatic frontman. Signed to the iconic Motown Records in 1969, their catalogue of hits, including "I Want You Back", "I'll Be There" and "ABC", sent them soaring to the top of the charts. With their snappy choreography and zingy, over-the-top costumes, the band were an instant hit with pop fans across the globe, with a young Michael's vocal gymnastics and cool dance moves standing out. Although the band never officially broke up, their success was lessened when Michael began his solo career in the early 70s.

Iconic Moment
The Monkees TV Series

When the Monkees burst on to our UK screens in 1967, a gazillion teenagers stared goggle-eyed at their TV's, barely able to believe what they were seeing: a wild and hilarious sitcom about the adventures of four young men trying to make a name for themselves as a pop band, playing catchy tunes like "Daydream Believer" and "Last Train To Clarksville" and generally mucking about. It was an instant hit. Not bad for a project only started as an American response to the Beatles (that even went on to outsell the Beatles). The Monkees, the manufactured pop band created for the show, became an overnight pop sensation. Did we care when it was later discovered that they didn't write or perform their own music, except to provide the vocals? Nope. The show and resulting pop icons were such an antidote to the bland TV of the era, it was only ever going to be a huge success.

60s

PAUL McCARTNEY

Jackie THE STONES

Jackie DAVE DEE etc.

Jackie ELVIS

Q and A
with Leo Sayer

"I Still Love Performing For An Audience!"

Q YOU'RE STILL TOURING AND WRITING. IS IT THE SAME THRILL AS IT WAS IN THE 70S?

A I still absolutely love it! Performing is what it's all about. I find myself completely focused on it now. The thrill of getting up on a stage and performing for an audience will never get old.

Q WHAT ARE YOUR MEMORIES OF "JACKIE" MAGAZINE?

A Well, it was the main magazine, wasn't it? I remember being featured in it alongside David Bowie, David Soul and David Essex! And when I performed at concerts, girls would bring along the pin-up posters of me from "Jackie" magazine for me to sign. I remember you also liked to ask things in interviews like, "What's your favourite colour?" Well, it was blue then . . . and it's still blue!

> Singer/songwriter Leo Sayer has kept us dancing since 1974! You can't stop a genuine star shining. We caught up with the cheery hit-maker and performer for a natter.

Q THE 70S WERE A BRILLIANT TIME FOR SONGS, WEREN'T THEY?

A Oh, yes! I loved writing songs with Roger Daltrey and others. You can't keep good music down. I live in Australia now and I was getting some work done on my house. The builder brought his 14-year-old son along. The young lad noticed my vinyl collection and immediately asked if I had any Led Zeppelin! The younger generation love all our stuff.

Q IF YOU COULD APPEAR IN A PHOTO STORY WITH ANYONE, WHO WOULD IT BE?

A Oh, that's a tricky one. I'll say Joni Mitchell . . . and my friend, Kate Bush.

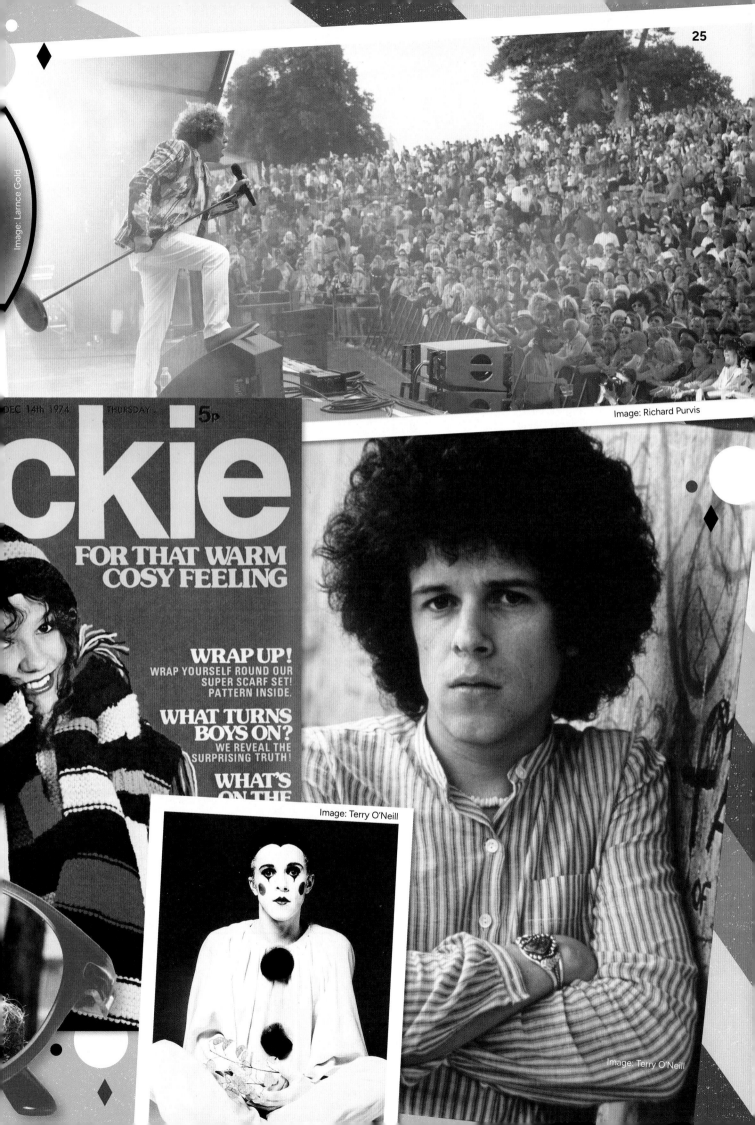

Image: Larnce Gold

Image: Richard Purvis

DEC 14th 1974   THURSDAY   5p

ckie
FOR THAT WARM COSY FEELING

WRAP UP!
WRAP YOURSELF ROUND OUR
SUPER SCARF SET!
PATTERN INSIDE.

**WHAT TURNS
BOYS ON?**
WE REVEAL THE
SURPRISING TRUTH!

**WHAT'S
ON THE**

Image: Terry O'Neill

Image: Terry O'Neill

MARC BOLAN

Marc Bolan epitomised the otherworldly pop star. With his unruly hair, glittery gold teardrops beneath his eyes and a penchant for topping off an outrageous outfit with a pink feather boa, he was a hero to the alternative kids who wanted something different from the clean cut, safe pop stars. Donny Osmond he was not! At the forefront of the glam rock movement, Marc and his band T. Rex stormed onto the scene with their breakthrough hit "Ride A White Swan" in 1970. From then until 1973 the band gave the Beatles a good run for their money, scoring 11 top 10 singles. Like his great rival and friend David Bowie, Marc became a master of reinvention, morphing through numerous fashion phases and tweaking his music to include disco, blues and soul with varying degrees of success. Sadly, his life was cut short when he died in a car crash in 1977.

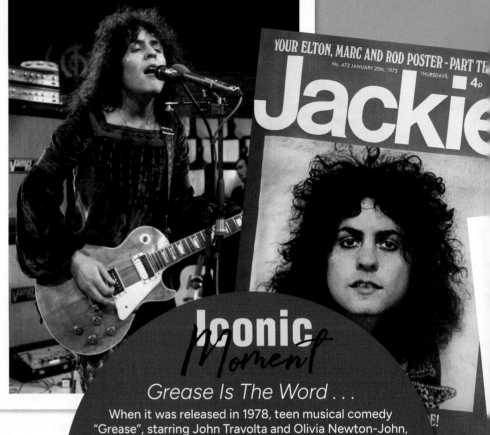

YOUR ELTON, MARC AND ROD POSTER - PART TH

No. 472 JANUARY 20th. 1973   THURSDAYS.   4p

Jackie

Iconic *Moment*

Grease Is The Word . . .

When it was released in 1978, teen musical comedy "Grease", starring John Travolta and Olivia Newton-John, was panned by the critics but became an instant hit with cinema goers. The boy-meets-girl summer romance story had a gaudy 1950s nostalgia and managed to perfectly capture the awkwardness and insecurities of those teenage years. The tunes were unforgettable. "Summer Nights", "Hopelessly Devoted To You", "You're The One That I Want" — every one had "Jackie" readers singing into their hairbrushes in their bedrooms, channelling their favourite Pink Lady, Marty, Frenchy or, for the more rebellious, Rizzo (gasp). "Grease" became an instant classic; even now, more than 40 years later when the film is wheeled out at Christmas, we embrace the nostalgia, recalling our own teenage years. The angst, the rebellion, bad haircuts — it's no wonder the film has had such an enduring afterlife.

DAVID ESSEX

David Essex didn't want to be a pop star; he wanted to be a professional football player and even got to train with West Ham as a teenager. But a passion for music soon took hold, the football boots were hung up and he pivoted to life as a singer and

actor, eventually breaking through to the mainstream when he won a part as Jesus in the hit musical "Godspell". This success led to "Rock On", his 1973 debut single which became a worldwide hit. He then penned and released one of his biggest hits "Gonna Make You A Star" which reached number one in the UK. David segued into movies, taking the lead role in "Stardust", and took on the part of Che in the London stage production of Andrew Lloyd Webber's "Evita". Latterly, he joined the cast of "EastEnders" for a stint as Eddie Moon.

Jackie

Music

70s

The decade of Cassidy, Bolan and Essex meant that the "Jackie" cover was never short of a heart-throb or two.

DAVID CASSIDY

Was there ever a bigger 1970s heart-throb than David Cassidy? We doubt it. The facts speak for themselves – "Jackie" magazine's best-ever selling issue was the 1972 special edition to coincide with his UK tour. It sold a whopping 1.1 million copies.

After rising to stardom in American musical sitcom "The Partridge Family", by the time he was 20, David was combining working on the TV show with creating solo albums. While he was wildly popular around the world, it was in the UK rather than his native America that he gained the most success. As someone who struggled with being a teen idol constantly under the spotlight (at its peak his fan club received 25,000 letters a week), he decided to quit acting and touring. Instead he concentrated on songwriting and releasing singles and albums, and, latterly, Broadway and West End musicals, all of which gave him continued success until his untimely death in 2017.

THE OSMONDS

One of the biggest "screamibopper" bands to come out of the US, The Osmonds were a Mormon five-member family band blessed with gorgeous looks, a squeaky-clean image and perfect, pearly white teeth. Originally a barber-shop quartet, they were later joined by Donny and it was then that they hit the pop jackpot. From their first hit "One Bad Apple" through to the distinctive "Crazy Horses" and "Love Me For A Reason", they sold over 77 million records and were even given their own cartoon series. And when chubby cheeked Little Jimmy Osmond joined the group to sing "Long Haired Lover From Liverpool", well, the whole world melted. The band's peak lasted until 1975 after which Donny, the most photogenic brother, whose face made many appearances on the cover of "Jackie" magazine, achieved a slew of solo hits including "The Twelfth Of Never", "Go Away Little Girl" and the unforgettably swoonworthy "Puppy Love".

ABBA

Originally called Björn & Benny, Agnetha & Anni-Frid, ABBA thankfully shortened their group's name to an acronym of their first names and wowed Europe in the 1974 Eurovision Song Contest with "Waterloo" (their second bite of the competition's cherry as the previous year they came third). While the supposed stigma of winning Eurovision affected their ability to be taken seriously for a while, ABBA eventually followed their monster hit with "SOS". From then on hit after hit flowed, from "Dancing Queen" to "Money, Money, Money", "Take A Chance On Me" and "Fernando", leading them to occupy the UK number one spot nine times between 1974 and 1980. After this point, however, they wrote and performed together less and less. Although ABBA never officially split, and despite the fervent hopes of their many fans, there has so far never been a live reunion.

Iconic *Moment*

The Sex Pistols: BANNED!

Punk rockers the Sex Pistols sparked outrage in 1977 when they released "God Save The Queen", an incendiary single that rebelled against the monarchy in the Queen's Silver Jubilee year. With its anti-establishment lyrics and decidedly disrespectful single sleeve, within days the BBC had banned it for being in "gross bad taste". Their appearance on broadcaster Bill Grundy's "Today" programme then became one of the most notorious interviews of all time. Littered with swear words and disintegrating into an out-of-control television segment, in the two and a half minutes it lasted, it helped put the sub-culture that was punk firmly in the mainstream. Although "God Save The Queen" was banned from being sold in shops like Woolworths, it still reached number 2 in the UK charts, though pipped to the top spot by a much more mellow tune – Rod Stewart's "I Don't Want To Talk About It".

BAY CITY ROLLERS

It took nine years for Scotland's original boy band to have a hit. Although formed by brothers Alan and Derek Longmuir in the mid-1960s, it wasn't until 1974 that the Bay City Roller's "Shang-A-Lang" got to number two in the pop charts and sent five lads from Edinburgh stratospheric. Hailed as the biggest thing since the Beatles, a string of hits followed, including a cover of the Four Seasons' "Bye Bye Baby" which sold 75,000 copies a day and stayed at number one for six weeks. And so it was that Rollermania began. Known for their tartan fashion and too-short trousers, the band sold 120 million records, had their own TV series and even conquered America, causing mass hysteria wherever they went and followed obsessively by tartan-clad teenage girls. Lead singer Les McKeown was a much screamed over regular on the cover of "Jackie" magazine, although the Rollers' popularity had waned by the late 70s.

To Jackie
Happy Valentines Day
Love,
Donny Osmond

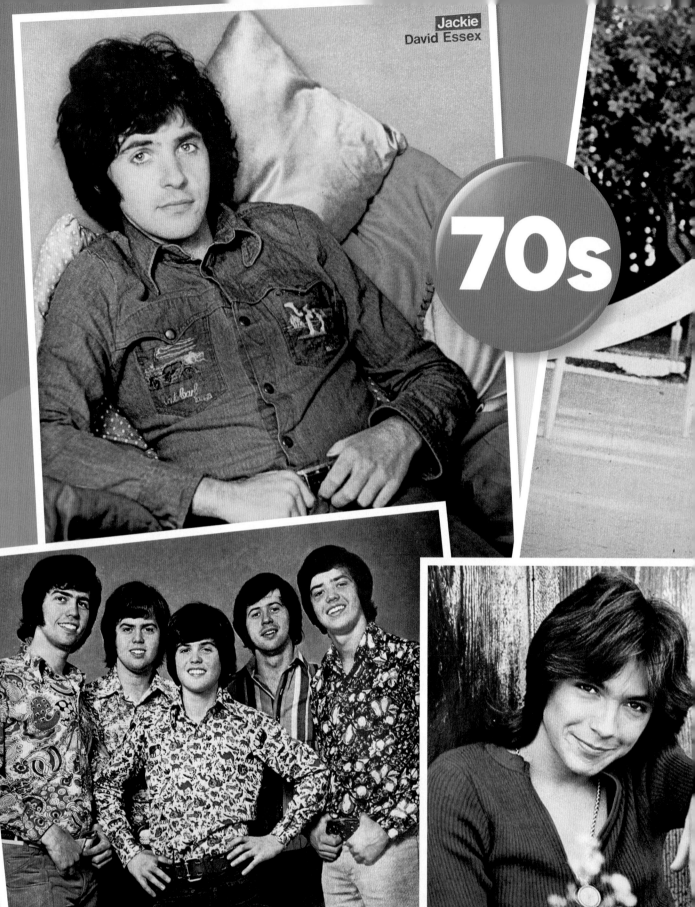

70s

jackie BeeGees

Q and A
with Fiction Factory

Back in 1984 when we were going to see "Ghostbusters", "Beverly Hills Cop" and "Police Academy", we were also singing along to the ever-wonderful "Feels Like Heaven" by Fiction Factory! We caught up with lead singer Kevin Patterson to reminisce about "Top Of The Pops" and appearing in a "Blue Jeans" photo story.

Q TELL US ABOUT YOUR TIME IN FICTION FACTORY!

A It was a four-part mini-series.
Episode 1: before we signed our record deal, everything seemed possible.
Episode 2: after we signed, everything seemed possible but only if the record company agreed it was.
Episode 3: when we were dropped, everything seemed possible again but far fewer people were interested.
Episode 4: after we released a second album, we ran out of steam.

Q WHAT WAS IT LIKE APPEARING ON "TOP OF THE POPS"?

A To be on a television show that I'd watched for years and on which every noteworthy artist had appeared, I felt a bit like one of those cartoon characters that's been hit over the head with an anvil. And then I bumped into John Peel and was so overawed I couldn't say anything intelligent! So it kind of felt like I was in a daze both times we did it.
   And then some singer I'd never heard of before called Madonna came and recorded a performance of "Holiday". I often wonder what happened to her.

Q WHO DID YOU GET TO MEET THAT REALLY IMPRESSED YOU?

A Alan Rankine, who was one half of The Associates. We worked with him on a song called "All Or Nothing" and his musicianship and musicality were literally breathtaking.

Q WHO WERE YOUR FAVOURITE BANDS AND SINGERS GROWING UP?

A My first two major favourites were Sparks and a band called Be Bop Deluxe. Then I discovered Kraftwerk and shortly after that came punk! That altered my entire thinking about music and performing, and set me off on a different direction. That's when three names appear: Magazine, The Slits, and Ultravox! – note the exclamation mark at the end . . . that's very important because, when they dropped it, they weren't good any more.

Q YOU'VE APPEARED IN A PHOTO STORY! WHO WOULD YOU MOST LIKE TO APPEAR IN A PHOTO STORY WITH NOW?

A Nigel Farage and Boris Johnson. It would be set on a boat in the middle of the Pacific Ocean and I wouldn't really feature very much. Just at the beginning, when I waved them off.

Q WHAT DO YOU DO NOW?

A I work in IT at the University of Dundee.

Q ARE YOU STILL IN TOUCH WITH ANYONE FROM THOSE YEARS?

A No, but no one from those years is in touch with me either!

Jackie

Music

80s

Outrageous hair, extravagant make-up... and magical, distinctive pop. Our music round-up ends in the glittering 80s.

WHAM!

Best friends from their time at school together, confident, outgoing Andrew Ridgeley was the perfect foil for shy Georgios Panayiotou. As teenagers the inseparable pair began writing songs together, eventually forming Wham! in 1981.

"Wham! Rap", the debut single released in 1982, was not an initial success. It was only when they were offered a last-minute slot on Top Of The Pops for their second release "Young Guns (Go For It!)" that they caught the attention of fans and their popularity soared. Known for their exuberant, uplifting tunes, Wham! became one of the most successful pop acts of the decade, selling more than 30 million records and the teen screaming shared equally between George and Andrew.

The band disbanded in 1986, primarily because songwriter George was keen to develop music targeted at a more grown-up audience, but the pair stayed close until George's untimely death on Christmas Day, 2016.

DURAN DURAN

Along with Spandau Ballet, the Eurythmics and The Human League, Duran Duran were at the forefront of the early 80s New Romantic movement, sporting floppy hair, flamboyant, eccentric fashion and music that relied heavily on the use of synthesisers. They were the epitome of pretty-boy pop and their army of Duranies adored them. John Taylor – all chiselled cheekbone and delicate features – was a particular fan favourite and it was he who appeared on the cover of "Jackie" more than most. With their blend of good looks and an innate ability to carve instant hits ("Rio", "Girls On Film", "Save A Prayer" and many more) they bossed the charts from 1981 until 1986. That was when Andy Taylor and Roger Taylor left the band due to exhaustion and tensions within the group. Although there were several other iterations in the line-up, Duran Duran never quite hit the same heady heights again, although they still perform today.

BANANARAMA

In 1980 Sarah Dallin and Keren Woodward, schoolmates from Bristol, joined up with Siobhan Fahey to share a flat together in London. All three were 18 years old, devoted to the club scene and had a desire to be famous. They took the name Bananarama in part from a favourite Roxy Music single, "Pyjamarama", and began turning out a slew of catchy hits including "It Ain't What You Do (It's The Way That You Do It", "Shy Boy" and "Venus". Having been keen followers of the post-punk music scene, their look was edgy; they wore bovver boots and had a ramshackle though heavily stylised fashion sense that the cool kids aspired to. If they were at your school, they would have surely been part of the "in" crowd, always slightly untouchable and a bit scary. Although Fahey left the group in the late 80s, Bananarama still perform as a duo.

Iconic Moment

Do They Know It's Christmas?

When Bob Geldof tuned into a BBC news report about the tragic effects of famine in Ethiopia, the Boomtown Rats frontman was so devastated by what he witnessed he vowed to do something. He and friend Midge Ure from Ultravox wrote charity record "Do They Know It's Christmas?" together and went through their respective address books, calling up every star they knew to meet in London one Sunday morning to record the single, all the while not quite knowing who would turn up. Fortunately, some of the biggest names in music obliged, including Bono from U2, George Michael, Sting, Spandau's Tony Hadley and Boy George. The resulting single went to number one in the charts, stayed there for five weeks and raised £8 million for Ethiopia within a year, surpassing all expectations. This wasn't enough to appease Geldof though, so he set about organising the biggest fundraising initiative of all time, Live Aid.

MADONNA

The original Queen of Pop burst into our lives in 1983 with her first hit single "Holiday", quickly followed by the more controversial "Like A Virgin", which came complete with a brassy video that added to the hype. Madonna has been a trailblazer ever since. Never afraid to reinvent herself or be controversial (her "Like A Prayer" video was condemned by the Vatican) but always pumping out the hits at high speed, she was at the forefront of pop for decades. While she rarely gave interviews (and never to teen magazines) she was nonetheless adored by a legion of fans who likened her to the provocative school rebel who broke the rules, dyed their hair and got told off for wearing their skirt too short. Intimidating, a control freak and the woman who put the capital 'S' in sass, most people agree there will never be another star like Madge.

JASON DONOVAN

Although he initially found fame as Scott Robinson in Australian soap "Neighbours", it wasn't until he began a career in music in 1988 that Jason Donovan became box office gold. His Aussie beach boy good looks, coupled with a cheeky demeanour and honeyed vocals, melted the hearts of pop fans everywhere. It was no surprise that his face adorned the walls of teenagers' bedrooms up and down the land. His debut album "Ten Good Reasons" was the UK's biggest selling record in 1989 and when he got together with fellow "Neighbours" star and even bigger pop poppet Kylie Minogue for "Especially For You", the pairing created pop dynamite. Not content with a music career, Jason also took on theatre roles in London's West End and beyond with his Olivier-award nominated lead role in "Joseph And His Amazing Technicolor® Dreamcoat", one of the most successful musical revivals of all time.

Iconic Moment
Live Aid

Not satisfied with organising the 1984 Christmas number one, Bob Geldof aimed even higher in his quest to raise funds for Ethiopian famine relief. He took an idea from Boy George who suggested a benefit concert and ran with it, going onto to organise a dual concert in London and America in July 1985. With less than a month of preparation, Geldof secured the services of an impressive array of artists, although this involved a certain amount of bluffing on Geldof's part – he told David Bowie that Elton John and Queen had agreed to play (at the time, they hadn't) and vice versa. It worked. The eventual line-up featured U2, Elton John and of course, the highlight of the show, Queen in the UK, along with Madonna and Mick Jagger in the US. The event drew in 1.5 billion television viewers and raised over £94 million (over £276 million in 2024 terms) in famine relief for African nations.

BROS

When twin brothers Matt and Luke Goss, along with friend Craig Logan (cruelly called "the other one" as he loitered in the shadows of two much bigger personalities) hit the charts with their aptly named breakthrough second single "When Will I Be Famous?", they started a mid-80s teen frenzy and an army of Brosettes sprang up overnight.

As well as good looks and catchy tunes like "I Owe You Nothing" and "Drop the Boy", the trio were known for their distinctive style of ripped Levi jeans and Grolsch bottle tops attached to their shoes. Brosmania swept the country, so much so that at the height of their fame the band had more than six million fan club members.

Although Craig left in 1989 due to illness, the twins carried on until 1992 when they too parted ways, briefly reuniting in 2017 for a concert and a much lauded documentary, "Bros: After the Screaming Stops".

Silly STAR FILE

NAME: Boy George O'Dowd. The name came about because it said on my birth certificate: Sex: Boy, George O'Dowd.

NICKNAME: Gorgeous George. I hate it!

DATE OF BIRTH: 14.6. 61.

FAMILY: Mother, father, four brothers and one sister.

HEIGHT: 5 ft. 11 in.

WHAT DID YOU HAVE FOR BREAKFAST? Today I had a cheese roll (brown bread, of course), and a cup of tea, though usually I have a bowl of bran flakes.

WHO WOULD YOU MOST LIKE TO BE STRANDED ON A DESERT ISLAND WITH? John Moss, who is one of the people in Culture Club.

WHO WOULD YOU LEAST LIKE TO BE STRANDED ON A DESERT ISLAND WITH? The Press Office of my record company – or a telephone.

WHAT'S THE FIRST THING YOU PUT ON WHEN YOU GET UP IN THE MORNING? My dressing gown.

PHOBIAS: I hate spiders and wasps. Whenever I see them I stamp on them.

HOW MANY PRESS-UPS CAN YOU MANAGE? Eugh! I don't like fitness!

WHAT'S THE SILLIEST ITEM OF CLOTHING YOU'VE EVER WORN? A pair of white stilettos.

VICES: My worst vice is falling in love.

HAVE YOU EVER BEEN IN HOSPITAL? Yes, but only for about five minutes to have a tetanus injection. Believe it or not, I've never actually been ill.

WHAT WOULD YOU DO WITH ONE DAY TO LIVE? If somebody told me that I only had one day to live I'd probably die of shock so I wouldn't have any time left to work out what to do.

ANYTHING YOU'D LIKE TO TELL THE WORLD? Yes. I went to school with Jeremy from Haysi Fantayzee, and I knew him when he used to look like an accountant!

Boy George with Culture Club drummer **John Moss.**

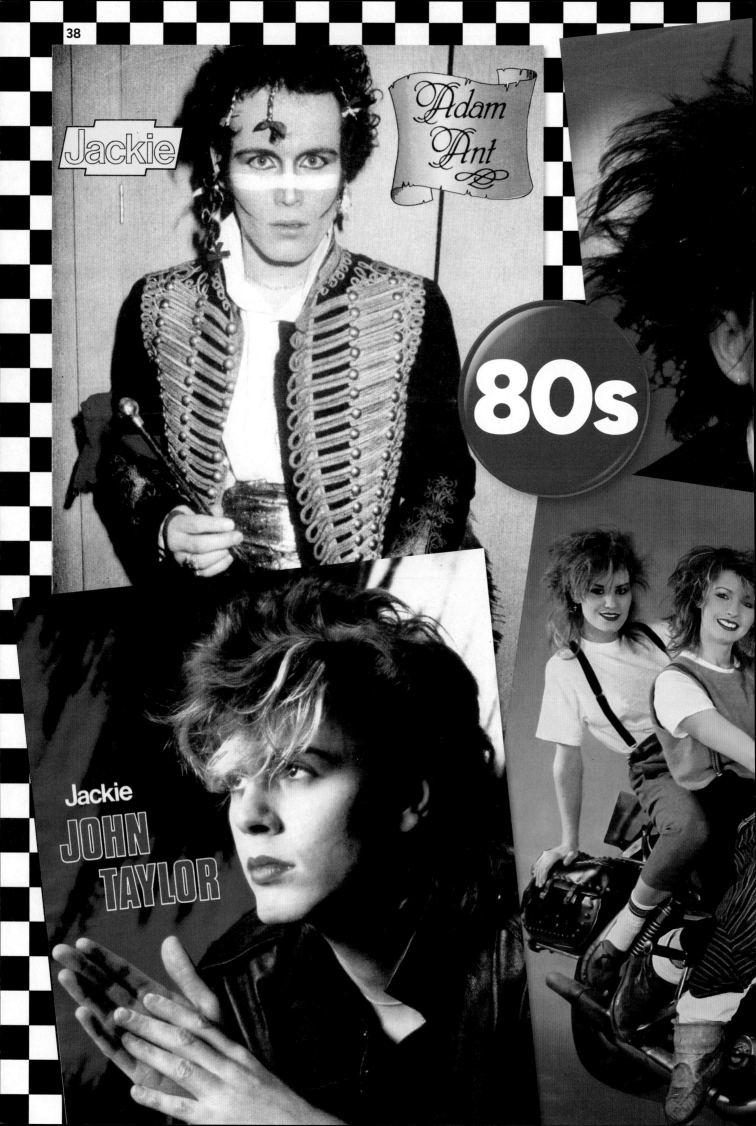

Jackie

Adam Ant

80s

Jackie
JOHN TAYLOR

JACKIE

KYLIE MINOGUE
SHOT: MUSIK & SHOW

Jackie

RICK ASTLEY

JACKIE

Q and A with Clare Grogan

Q DID YOU READ "JACKIE" MAGAZINE IN YOUR TEENAGE YEARS?

A Absolutely . . . didn't everyone!

Q DID YOU EVER THINK YOU WOULD APPEAR IN THE PAGES?

A No. But that is the beauty of life, you never know what might happen.

Q WHAT ARE YOUR FAVOURITE MEMORIES FROM THE 1980S?

A Discovering music and movies I really identified with. Touring with Altered Images, Making "Gregory's Girl" and making lifelong friends as a result. Falling in love with my husband Stephen. Living in New York for a while . . . it was an action-packed decade for me.

Q HOW EXCITING WAS IT TO APPEAR ON "TOP OF THE POPS"?

A Very exciting and also terrifying. It all happened pretty much overnight for me. It really was a dream come true moment. I was always awestruck in the Green Room — lots of my favourite artists were there, most of whom I was too shy to talk to.

Q DID YOU EVER WRITE TO CATHY AND CLAIRE?

A No, but my friends and I loved reading those problems. We learned stuff in between giggling.

Q WHICH POSTERS DID YOU HAVE ON YOUR WALL WHEN YOU WERE A TEENAGER?

A Audrey Hepburn, Judy Garland, James Dean, David Essex, David Bowie, Debbie Harry, Siouxsie and the Banshees. I had quite eclectic taste.

Q WHO WOULD YOU MOST LIKE TO APPEAR IN A PHOTO STORY WITH?

A Great question! I'd have to say Matt Dillon, my favourite member of the Brat Pack. I still love him.

Q ARE YOU STILL IN TOUCH WITH ANY FELLOW STARS FROM THE 1980S?

A Lots of them. The never-ending 80s revival brings us together quite a lot.

This summer I've played Festivals with the Human League, Kim Wilde, Heaven 17, Toyah, Tony Hadley . . . I could go on and on.

Altered Images

Performing at Let's Rock Leeds 80s Festival 2024

Altered Images featured in "Jackie" magazine
No. 974 (September 4, 1982)

Silly STARFILE

CLARE GROGAN, ALTERED IMAGES

NAME: Clare Patricia Grogan.
DATE OF BIRTH: 17.3.1962.
HEIGHT: 5 ft. 2½ ins.
FAMILY: Two sisters, Kate and Margaret.
WHAT DID YOU DREAM LAST NIGHT? I dreamt I was being attacked by a monster rat. It was horrible.
NASTIEST HABIT: Mimicking people.
WHAT SORT OF THINGS ANNOY YOU ABOUT OTHER PEOPLE? Noisy eaters.
FAVOURITE UNDERWEAR: My Long-Johns.
SILLIEST FAN LETTER: All those proposals of marriage. One boy keeps sending me gold bracelets and watches. I've written to ask him to stop it but he carries on sending them anyway.
IF YOU COULD HAVE ONE LUXURY, WHAT WOULD YOU CHOOSE? My own hairdresser.
HAVE YOU EVER BEEN IN HOSPITAL? I've never had to stay in overnight but I've been in several times to have bumps and grazes seen to. When we were on "Swap Shop," our guitarist, Tony, knocked me out with his guitar and they took me to hospital in a wheelchair.
WHAT'S THE SILLIEST ITEM OF CLOTHING YOU'VE EVER WORN? I once wore men's silk pyjamas during a concert and nobody even realised. They all thought it was something I'd had specially designed!
IF YOU COULD BE SOMEBODY ELSE, WHO WOULD YOU CHOOSE? Rebecca, the heroine of Daphne Du Maurier's novel
WHO WOULD YOU MOST LIKE TO BE STRANDED ON A DESERT ISLAND WITH? Richard Gere.
WHO WOULD YOU LEAST LIKE TO BE STRANDED WITH? Denis Thatcher.
BEST SUBJECT AT SCHOOL: History.
WORST SUBJECT: Latin.
DO YOU SING IN THE BATH? I sing everywhere — mostly songs I don't particularly like, from musicals.

No. 974 SEPTEMBER 4, 1982   THURSDAYS   16p IR 24½p

Jackie

INSIDE FREE

FIRST OFF
PERFORM
Bristows
DEEP SHINE

FANTASTIC SHAMPOO
& CONDITIONER for
super shiny hair!

PLUS
2 MONEY-OFF
VOUCHERS!

sensational
SHAKY
pin-up!

exclusive
ALTERED IMAGES
photo feature!

Jackie GO TO YOUR HEAD TODAY!

JANUARY

1. **"Imagine" by John Lennon reached number one in January '81. In what year was it first released as a single?**
2. Bucks Fizz were number one in January '82 with "Land Of Make Believe" but what was the name of the song they won the Eurovision song contest with?
3. **David Soul had a hit with "Don't Give Up On Us" in January '77. What was the name of the famous police show he starred in on television?**
4. The Pretenders had a January hit with "Brass In Pocket". What were the names of the original Pretenders?
5. **Shakin' Stevens changed his name by deed poll when he had a hit with "Oh Julie" in January '82, but what was his real name?**
6. Can you identify this song by the lyrics?
   "I light a candle to our love, In love our problems disappear But all in all we soon discover, That one and one is all we long to hear"
7. **In January 1979 Village People had a number one hit with YMCA. Which "village" did the group refer to?**

Ultimat

Image: Alamy

APRIL

1. **In April 1982 Paul McCartney had a hit single with Stevie Wonder. What was it called?**
2. The Detroit Spinners had a number one with "Working My Way Back To You" in April '82. What were they originally called?
3. **Mike Batt wrote Art Garfunkel's "Bright Eyes". Who had he previously written songs for?**
4. Which famous person was the song "Matchstalk Men And Matchstalk Cats And Dogs" written about?
5. **The Bay City Rollers had a number one hit in April '74 with "Bye Bye Baby". Can you name the only other number one hit they had?**

MAY

1. **Boney M had a hit in May '78 with "Rivers Of Babylon". What was the name of the B side of this record which was also a big hit for them?**
2. This song was a major hit in May '83. Can you recognise it and the singer by these lyrics?
   "If you say run I'll run with you, And if you say hide we'll hide.
   Because my love for you would break my heart in two, If you should fall into my arms and tremble like a flower."
3. **The first ever number one to include a day of the week in the title was by Blondie in May '79. Can you name it?**
4. Dexy's Midnight Runners had their first hit with "Geno". Who was this song a tribute to?
5. **Adam And The Ants had a hit in May' 81 with "Stand and Deliver" but do you know Adam Ant's real name?**

FEBRUARY

1. **"Don't Cry For Me; Argentina"** was a number one hit for Julie Covington in February 1977. Which successful musical was it taken from?
2. The Chrysalis label scored its first number one hit with "When I Need You". Who sang it?
3. **Joe Dolce had a hit with "Shaddup You Face" in February '81, but do you know what he called the "character" he played while singing it?**
4. The Jam's second single went straight in at number one with "A Town Called Malice/Precious" in February '82. What was their first single to do this?
5. **What was the name of the album that John Lennon's "Woman" came from?**
6. Michael Jackson had a hit in February '83 with "Billie-Jean." Lydia Murdock sang a follow up single – what was it called?
7. **Kajagoogoo had a hit with "Too Shy" before they sacked their lead singer. What was his name?**

MARCH

1. Kate Bush had a smash hit with "Wuthering Heights," but who wrote the classic novel by the same name?
2. In March '79 The Bee Gees had a hit single called "Tragedy". Shortly before this they had a smash hit with the soundtrack of a film. This was the best selling album of all time until it was knocked off its pedestal by "Thriller". What was it called?
3. **In March 1981, Roxy Music was number one with "Jealous Guy". The only words printed on the sleeve of this single were the title, the artist and the phrase "a tribute". Who was it a tribute to?**
4. Tight Fit had a hit in March '82 with a cover track. It is the only number one to have as six names on the writing credits. What was it called?
5. **The Goombay Dance Band had a hit with "Seven Tears" in '82. What, apart from singing, is the frontman Oliver Bendt famous for?**
6. Which album did the Thompson Twins' single "Love On Your Side" come from?

Pop Quiz

Well, here it is – the big quiz you've all been waiting for! So are you a pop egghead, Miss Average or simply clueless? Give yourself one point for each correct answer, then add them up to find out your score...

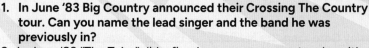

JUNE

1. **In June '83 Big Country announced their Crossing The Country tour. Can you name the lead singer and the band he was previously in?**
2. In June '83 "The Tube" did a five-hour summer spectacular with Paula Yates as a co-presenter of. She once brought out a book of photographs called -
a) Rock Stars In Their Underpants b) Rock Stars In Their Socks c) Rock Stars In The Flesh
3. **"Are 'Friends' Electric?" was a hit for Tubeway Army in June '79. What is odd about this?**
4. What was the name of the group who had a hit with "Candy Girl"?
5. **The Wurzels had a hit with "Combine Harvester (Brand New Key)." What year was it released?**

Ultimate 80s Pop Quiz

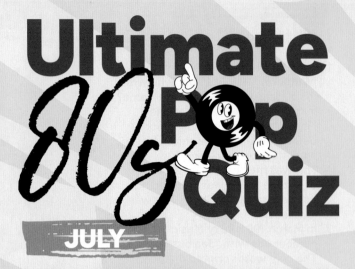

JULY

1. John Travolta and Olivia Newton-John had a hit with "You're The One That I Want." What other track sung by them from the film "Grease" reached number one?
2. A story heard over the radio prompted a young man to write a song. A teenage Californian had shot at her playground friends causing death and injury. What is the name of the song and what band sang it?
3. The Specials reached number one in July '81 with "Ghost Town". Subsequently they split up. What band was formed by three member of the Specials?
4. Can you name the band and its members who had a hit with "Bad Boys" in July '83?
5. "Every move you make, Every step you take, Every claim you stake, I'll be watching you." Can you name this song and who sang it?

AUGUST

1. A Scottish folk singer, Mary Sandeman, had a one-off hit in August '81 with "Japanese Boy". What was the name she used instead of her own when she recorded the track?
2. David Bowie continued the story of Major Tom in August 1980 with "Ashes To Ashes". It was not a great hit in the U.S. but Bowie scored an even bigger hit in the lead role of a play. What was it called?
3. Twenty years and 25 days after his first number one hit, Cliff Richard did it again in August '79. What was the name of the record?
4. Can you name the singer and song with these lyrics, which was a hit in August '83?
"By the look in your eyes
I can tell you're gonna cry,
Is it over me?
If it is save your tears,
'Cos I'm not worth it, you'll see"
5. Soft Cell reached number one in '81 with "Tainted Love". Which record label did they record it with?
6. Who was the "fairy godmother" in the video for Adam And The Ants' "Prince Charming" single?

OCTOBER

1. Lesley Gore sang "It's My Party" in 1963. Who was it a hit for in October '81?
2. Can you name the L.P. which featured Culture Club's "Karma Chameleon"?
3. Tina Turner made a comeback in December '83. Who was the other half of the famous duo she sang with several years before that?
4. Rod Stewart had his biggest ever hit in October '71. What was it called?
5. "Video Killed The Radio Star" was a hit for which group in 1979?

NOVEMBER

1. Identify the song and the group from these lyrics:
"I wanna be your number one, number one.
I'm not the kind of girl who gives up just like that."
2. Which band did David Bowie have a number one hit with in November '81 called "Under Pressure"?
3. Dr Hook had a number one with "When You're In Love With A Beautiful Woman" in November of in which year?
4. What is the nationality and name of the band who had a hit with "Rat Trap" in November '78?
5. What kind of girl did Billy Joel sing about in November '83?

SEPTEMBER

1. In September '78 there was another hit in the charts from the film "Grease" but do you know which characters Olivia Newton-John and John Travolta played?
2. Which single by The Police followed up their "Message In A Bottle" hit?
3. A young girl from Paisley in Scotland went to number one with her first single "Feels Like I'm In Love" in September 1980. What was she called?

WOW!

DECEMBER

1. Which well-known heavy metal group had a Christmas Number one in 1973 with "Merry Christmas Everybody"?
2. The Flying Pickets had a Christmas hit with a cover version of "Only You". Which band first sang this?
3. What was the name of Showaddywaddy's smash hit in December '76?
4. Paul Young re-released his single "Love Of The Common People" at Christmas time in 1983. It reached number 3. What were his backing singers called?
5. Who had a hit with "There's No-One Quite Like Grandma"?
6. The Police had their second chart topper with "Walking On The Moon" in December '79. Which album was it taken from?
7. Pink Floyd had a huge hit with an anti-education anthem. What was it called?
8. The only single that sold a million copies in '81 was by the Human League. What was it?
9. "Mull Of Kintyre" was number one in December '77. What was the B-side called?

ANSWERS

JANUARY
1 1975 2 Making Your Mind Up 3 Starsky And Hutch 4 Chrissie Hynde, James Honeyman-Scott, Pete Farndon and Martin Chambers 5 Michael Barrat 6 Pipes Of Peace by Paul McCartney 7 Greenwich Village in New York

FEBRUARY
1 Evita 2 Leo Sayer 3 Giuseppi 4 Going Undergroud 5 Double Fantasy 6 Superstar 7 Limahl

MARCH
1 Emily Bronte 2 Saturday Night Fever 3 John Lennon 4 The Lion Sleeps Tonight 5 Fire-eating 6 Quick Step 8 Side Kick

APRIL
1 Ebony And Ivory 2 The Motown Spinners 3 The Wombles 4 L. S. Lowry 5 Give A Little Love

MAY
1 Brown Girl in The Ring 2 Let's Dance, David Bowie 3 Sunday Girl 4 Geno Washington and his Ram Jam Band 5 Stuart Goddard

JUNE
1 Stuart Adamson, The Skids, 2 a. 3 It was sung by Gary Numan. The Tubeway Army was a thing of the past and he retained the name 4 New Edition 5 1976

JULY
1 Summer Nights 2 I Don't Like Mondays, The Boomtown Rats 3 Fun Boy Three 4 Wham!, Andrew Ridgely and George Michael 5 Every Breath You Take, The Police

AUGUST
1 Aneka 2 The Elephant Man 3 We Don't Talk Anymore 4 Paul Young, Wherever I Lay My Hat (That's My Home) 5 Phonogram 6 Diana Dors

SEPTEMBER
1 Danny and Sandy 2 Roxanne 3 Kelly Marie

OCTOBER
1 Dave Stewart with Barbara Gaskin 2 Colour By Numbers 3 Ike Turner 4 Maggie May 5 The Buggles

NOVEMBER
1 The Tide is High, Blondie 2 Queen 3 1979 4 Irish, Boomtown Rats 5 Uptown Girl

DECEMBER
1 Slade 2 Yazoo 3 Under The Moon Of Love 4 Maz Roberts and Kim Lesley 5 St Winifred's School Choir 6 Reggatta de Blanc 7 Another Brick in The Wall 8 Don't You Want Me? 9 Girls' School

CONCLUSIONS

55 - 68: All right, Smarty – you might as well admit it now-you cheated, didn't you?

30 - 54: Not bad, not bad at all, but we bet you had to look up your book of hit singles for half the answers.

15 - 29: This isn't so hot, is it? How often do you listen to the radio? Once a month? Once a year? Oh, I see – never.

Under 15: Aw, c'mon. Where have you been hiding for the past few years? Oh sorry, didn't realise you were still into Barry Manilow.

FASHION AND *Beauty*

FOR several generations of girls, leaving the house was not possible without having looked through the latest issue of "Jackie" magazine. Why? Quite simply, it was the ultimate style bible to have you looking and feeling great, whether you were going for a Coke with your friends, or trying to look your best for that all-important first date with the boy of your dreams.

"Jackie" became the place to go for tips on all the latest trends. Every issue included fashion shoots, which were eye-catching and imaginative.

"Jackie" staff would regularly head off on their travels, creating wonderful spreads that never failed to inspire.

You would never be short of an idea of what to wear and how to wear it!

For young girls, learning to put on their make-up is a rite of passage, and here "Jackie" was a thoughtful, creative teacher.

Beauty tips for all occasions frequently cropped up and, as always, the sage advice was presented in an accessible and delightful way.

Girls would pass copies between their friends, sharing hints and ideas.

Some features were exotic, some were more down to earth, but they all had one thing in common — they were works of art and "Jackie" girls everywhere would lap them up!

Over the next few pages, we remember some classic spreads...

TOP KNOT TIME–this week it's

ROMANCEVILLE

It's chic to look beat in the daytime—but it's great to be swish around date-time!

This week's hair-do is soft and feminine. You're going to love it—and that goes for your fella, too.

The step-by-step diagrams are given below.

and here's how you do it

styled by Parr's Salons

TOP KNOT TIME–this week it's

THE TRENDSTER

This week's style rates the most, 'cos it's a cinch to keep neat 'n' cute. It's pert and casual and comes in out of the wind looking great!

Remind you of anybody? Maybe John, or Paul, or George, or Ringo?

and here's how you do it

TOP KNOT TIME–this week it's

Imp Flip

and here's how you do it

styled by Parr Salons

Jackie
Hairstyles

Throughout the 60s and 70s, "Jackie" readers were never short of hairstyle inspiration. When Friday night was looming and the lights of the disco were on the horizon, you just knew that "Jackie" would have the perfect look for you.

TOP KNOT TIME–this week it's

Carefree

Want to be cute 'n' chic? Add a gingham ribbon to a hairstyle with zing—and you're in!

All you do is follow the simple setting instructions below for a hairdo that's sure to catch that fella's eye—and interest.

and here's how you do it

styled by Parr's Salons.

TOP KNOT TIME–this week it's

Cilla

Who's the most Mod girl on the scene? Cilla!

So who's the most with it hairwise? Cilla!

and here's how you do it

Styled by Richard Henry, London and Rome.

TOP KNOT TIME
Golden Girl

Brush hair thoroughly when dry. Let right hand section fall over your cheek and flick forward into a curl. Brush left hand section back and flick out. Spray lightly.

Sunsilk Hairspray.

TOP KNOT TIME – this week it's

THE Petal

Every week, on this page, you'll get a zany, up-to-the-second style, specially created for you.
You'll earn yourself one-two-three glances—and top marks for being cute—when you step out on the town in this one.
It's a simple-to-set, all pin-curls style. Have fun! See you next week!

and here's how you do it

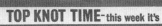

styled by Parr's Salons.

TOP KNOT TIME TAWNY GLOW

This style is best for girls with heavy hair. Set on very large rollers and pin curl as loosely as possible. Brush in direction of rollers and pin curls. Back brush the crown slightly, then spray lightly.

With thanks to Sunsilk Hairspray.

TOP KNOT TIME – this week it's
mod girl

How about this, then? Something pretty special—and really mod.
Strictly for female-type females, he-males are crazy about it.
Styled for you, with him in mind, try it out from the diagrams below and just wait for the wows!

and here's how you do it

styled by Parr's Salons.

TOP KNOT TIME – this week it's

Susan

Somethin' special—and slightly Spanish—about this. Susan Maughan designed it. Have fun!

and here's how you do it

TOP KNOT TIME – this week it's

Ginchy Girl

This is an easy-to-do style. Sleek 'n' chic—and it has a cheeky flickup.
Follow the diagrams below if you want to try it yourself. Or take it to your hairdresser and give yourself a treat!

and here's how you do it

styled by Parr's Salons.

TOP KNOT TIME – this week it's

Glow girl

When HE sees you wearing this hairstyle on a big date, girl, all the stops are out.
And it's a lot simpler to set than it looks. Follow the diagrams below—or ask your hairdresser to do it.
One word of warning, though. Don't wear this style unless you really fancy the guy. He'll flip—but really!

and here's how you do it

styled by Parr's Salons.

TOP KNOT TIME – this week it's

FANCY FREE

For the gal who's cute, yet has a yen for the sophisticated, this week's style will take you from wake-up time to live-it-up time.
Have fun trying it out from the diagrams below—and more fun still when admiring glances follow you. Hoots, and how about the dash of tartan?

and here's how you do it

styled by Parr's Salons.

Jackie *Beauty*

As every girl knows, the easiest way to look great is to exude happiness and confidence. With endless tips on all aspects of beauty, "Jackie" girls had all the ingredients to feel and look amazing all day, every day.

A JACKIE BEAUTY BOX

MAKING SUNNY FACES

A FACE in the sun looks healthy and glowing, but it isn't all plain sailing! Freckles, for instance, seem to be a common problem; flaking and burning aren't so nice either. And the time to keep your tan long-lasting and golden, instead of fading to a dingy yellow, is while you're sunning—not when it's already on the way out!

FRECKLE PHOBIAS

Let's start with freckles, because these seem to be a heart-break for many of you. Goodness knows why, because they can look absolutely super. But while lots of the model girls we know spend ages painting them on, many of you are going through agony because of them! So if we can't convince you they're nice, we'll try to help.

Firstly, there's nothing you can do to prevent freckles appearing when you go out in the sun, unless you use a cream such as Kerodex, by Innoxa, which screens out all the tanning or burning rays. This is used in much the same way as you use a tanning product, except that it has the opposite effect, of course. Costs around 38p.

Bleaching freckles which are actually there is not really to be recommended. It can be done with neat lemon juice or a very mild peroxide solution, but it's quite a pointless operation. Apart from the fact that you're drying your skin badly, the freckles will return again when you go out in the sun.

So it really is a question of camouflage. The choice is whether you try to hide the freckles, or merge them in by darkening the rest of your skin.

In summer, the latter is probably the best idea. So use either a fake tan, or a tan gel make-up for an instant bronzing which will disguise the freckles.

If you prefer a pale face, then you need a make-up containing plenty of pigment to cover the freckles. Leichner's Kamera Klear foundations in stick or tube do give excellent coverage. They cost 50p and 40p respectively.

Most stick make-ups also provide enough coverage — Max Factor's Pan Stick for example.

A dusting of translucent powder sets the camouflage well and keeps it in place longer.

Remember to cleanse very thoroughly when you wear fairly heavy make-up. It won't do you any harm if properly removed, but if left on, it could easily block your pores.

However, do take a fair and critical look at yourself in the mirror. Are your freckles really unattractive? It's far more likely that they make you look pert and pretty. So rather than try to hide them, show them off. They tend to look good with today's natural look—a proof that you're real!

And for those of you who are feeling freckle-less and neglected, here's how to paint them on! Dip a fine eyeliner brush in tan gel make-up. Max Factor's California Eye Gloss in bronze, a brown water shadow, or some very dark make-up. Dot freckles on either side of your nose and along the cheeks. This looks most natural—if you continue over the bridge of the nose and on the rest of your face, it becomes rather obvious they're fake.

DEGREES OF DRYNESS

In your eagerness to end up browner than anyone else, it is possible that you'll get badly burnt—despite all the warnings we hand out about lying too long in the sun!

In cases of really bad burns, it's wise to see a doctor, because you may need some treatment.

But for the normal type of sunburn—which is bad enough!—smooth on Histolax or a calomine lotion to soothe the skin.

Luckily, not all of us will scorch ourselves to this extent, but dryness can reach the stage of severe peeling. This means you'll not only look a bit strange for a while, but your tan is flaking off, too.

This is when you realise how important sun-screening oils, creams, etc, are. And especially on areas already prone to dryness, such as knees, elbows, and cheeks, and sensitive areas such as upper arms, neck, thighs, and shoulders.

However, if it's too late to think about that, but you haven't yet begun to peel, try a special moisturiser such as Nivea's After Sun Soother or Apres Soleil to keep the skin supple.

For skin that's already in a bad way, banish soap. Use a cream cleanser like Ponds Cold Cream, then a rich moisturiser such as Ponds Dry Skin Cream, Endocil, Novara, or Boots 17 All Rounder Cream.

All this nourishment ought to replace the oils which the sun has dried away.

Your body, too, needs care. Again, try to avoid the use of soap by using a cleansing bath gelee such as Femfresh, or a body shampoo like All Over Softly, which may or may not be available in your area yet.

To keep your skin supple, put a capful of baby oil in the water, and rub it into knees, elbows, or anywhere that feels rough and dry.

These same tactics will prolong your tan, even if you've escaped dryness and peeling. It's the tiny bit of skin that normal 'wear and tear' removes, which cause that faded look, so keep well-oiled!

If you go a horrid yellow colour after a few weeks, it's time to take action. Either keep the tan looking brown and healthy by using a fake tan on top, or make sure you quickly return to normal colour by using a face pack to speed up the process. These usually have a mildly bleaching effect.

HAIR SCARE

The other part of you that's likely to take quite a beating from the sun, is your hair. This can change overnight from shiny and swingy, to dull, dry and coarse. So be warned, and keep a sunhat firmly on your head if you're in hot sun.

For hair that is damaged, it's most important to bleach, perm, straighten, or colour until it's back to normal. Any of these treatments will make the condition even worse. Merely shampoo with a rich conditioning shampoo (Inecto's Peach Nut Oil, Living Hair Cream, Corimist or Sunsilk Protein are all good).

Condition with a good product like Beauty Countess, Inecto's Peach Nut Oil, Living Hair, Corimist or Sunsilk Protein.

Don't pull, tug, brush when wet, dry in great heat or tangle your hair by brisk towel rubs. Just squeeze the water out gently, and dry with a warm hair-dryer naturally, patting with a towel.

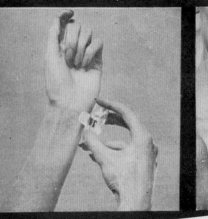

PERFUME

Perfume is the gilt to the lily, the blush of beauty to the rose—and every girl's built-in X-factor for luring the boy of her dreams.

The wise charmer knows the whys, hows and wherefores of a girl's most-proven ally.

The secret is little and often. Don't pour half a pint of perfume behind your ears in the morning and expect it to last all day. A little perfume on your pulse points in the morning and a touch up about every four hours at temple, throat and wrists during the day will make sure the fragrance never fades.

Try to have talc and toilet water to match your perfume for a delicious all-over fragrance.

Take a bottle of your fave pe... he-males, of course—dab a little o...

... on wrists ...

Lovely eyes—as quick as a wink!

If you want to make eyes at boys, make them eyes possible. Skilful eye make-up won't help make them look even heavier. But skilful ey... awake, bright 'n' beautiful look of ... Just eye-up these hints, practise them as ofter... that girl with the gorge...

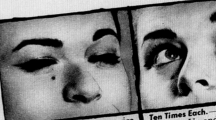

Rest Eyes Often.—Once or twice during the day close your eyes and move them left, right, upwards and downwards a few times behind your closed lids.

Ten Times Each.—R... exercises. Up and d... ment; left to righ... down from one cor... eye to the o...

BLACK MAGIC IN A BOTTLE

...d for the best effect—on ...owing pulse-points ...

...iest, most appealing ...ore eyes. In fact, it'll ...-up, plus that wide-...eyes—wow! ...can, and—say, who's ...?

Cleansing Eyes. — Never ...bed with eye make-up s ...There are special pads y ...buy that remove masca ...cleansing cream will ...as well.

SO YOU THINK MAKING UP IS HARD TO DO? WELL IT ISN'T!

Want to look great but don't know the first thing about make-up? We tell you what to buy and what to do with it . . . making up's easy when you know how!

WHAT TO BUY

YOU'VE probably got some bits and pieces lying about already . . . eye and lip colours you've bought for special occasions but thrown aside when you found they didn't look so good!

Making up's a simple step-by-step process, but it won't work properly if you miss out any of the steps. Buying the right things comes first . . . if you don't have the right materials to work with you can't possibly get the right sort of look. Here's what you need:

1. Skin care products.

As soon as you start to use make-up you'll need to take extra care of your skin, using a proper cleanser to remove all your make-up at the end of the day because soap and water won't do the job properly. Then you'll need a toner to remove any grease left on your face and tone up the pores of your skin and, finally, a moisturiser to keep your skin soft and supple.

You need moisturiser for protecting your skin during the day, too, and if you choose to use a foundation colour you'll find it's much easier to put on if you've used a moisturiser first.

Skin care products can be expensive, but there are some good ones to try that won't break the bank. There's the Boots 17 Skin Care range for instance with Herbal Cleanser, Toner and Moisturiser for greasy skin, and Orange Blossom for dry or normal skin. Evette also have a good range of products available at Woolworth branches.

You'll also need cotton wool for cleansing and toning. The synthetic kind is best (although it costs more). Those big rolls of real cotton wool tend to be bitty and harsher than the synthetic types.

2. Foundation.

This is the next step in the making up routine. Foundation creams and liquids give the skin an even tone, can cover little blemishes and also help to protect your skin during the day. The big mistake you might make with foundation is to buy a colour that's lighter or darker than your own skin tones — this just makes you look 'made-up'

and unnatural.

The colour you choose *must* be about the same as your own skin colour. Before buying a foundation, try a little on the back of your hand and also put a dot on your cheek . . . take a friend along with you to make sure you're choosing the right one.

Rimmel, Outdoor Girl, Boots 17, Evette all do good foundations at low prices. Try Rimmel's Liquid Make-Up, 32p, Boots 17 Near Skin, 35p, or Outdoor Girl Total finish, 42p.

3. Blusher

Blusher isn't just for adding colour to your cheeks . . . it helps to define cheek-bones, shape your face and make your eyes look bigger. With all those jobs to do, it's important to choose the colour and type that's best for you.

Cream blusher is easily applied with the finger-tips, while powder blusher should be applied with a brush . . . once you've mastered the brush you'll find that powder blusher stays on your cheeks longer.

Start off with a blusher like Rimmel Pressed Rouge, 23p, Cream Rouge, 19p, or Miners Cream Blusher, 22p, Tawny Powder Blusher, 22p. And if you choose the powder blusher, invest in a nice fat blusher brush. Boots do one for about 30p.

4. Eye Colours

Of all the eye shadows there are, pencils are probably the easiest to use. You can use them for drawing socket-lines between lids and brow-bones, for colouring in lids, highlighting, and for soft smudging under lower lashes and above upper ones.

If you want a special sparkly look for evenings, you'll need a powder shadow . . . that's the only type that *can* be sparkly.

Look for Miners Soft Eye Sticks, 20p, and their Magic Crayons, 32p, Boots 17 Eye Stix, 32p, or Rimmel's Jumbo Eye Shadow/Liner pencils, 49p.

5. Mascara.

When you choose a mascara you're looking for a number of things . . . good colour and texture — none of those annoying little bits that smudge on your cheeks and a good brush or applicator that doesn't clog up and is easy to use. Mascara makes your lashes look longer, thicker and darker and it finishes off the eye, especially when you're wearing eye make-up.

You can wear mascara by itself, of course, or with just a trace of shadow on lids for the natural look.

Good mascaras to try are Rimmel's Brush-On Lash Thickener, 42p, or the Block Mascara, 22p, Miners Big Build Up, 45p, Autobrush, 34p, or Block Mascara, 21p, also Outdoor Girl Marvelash, 45p.

6. Lip Colours

These are fairly straightforward. If you want a deep colour go for a proper lipstick, but if you just want a slick of colour, go for a lip gloss. A lip-brush is by far the best way to apply lip colour, you can define the edges, get into those corners and you'll find that the colour will last longer if you've used a lip-brush. Boots make a good lip-brush for just 22p.

Look for good lip colours in the Evette, Rimmel, Boots 17, Miners, Outdoor Girl, Tangee ranges.

HOW IT'S DONE

1. Foundation is applied over moisturiser. Let your moisturiser sink in for a minute or two, then take your foundation and put little dots of it all over your face and neck. Now blend it in with your fingertips using upward strokes, or use the tip of a slightly dampened sponge for blending for a really smooth finish. Make sure you blend evenly round chin and ears, no hard lines anywhere!

use powder blusher and a brush, use light strokes so the colour isn't too heavy.

2. Blusher comes next, over foundation. Find your cheek bones with your finger and thumb and start "blushing" from there, blending out to temples in a triangular shape. If you

3. Eyes. Use an eye pencil first of all to shade in the bone above the eye lid, out to the corners and round under the lower lashes. Use a brown or grey for this depending on your eye colour and the colour you'll be using on your lids.

Now fill in the lids with colour, remembering that *lighter* colours on lids will make your eyes look bigger, *darker* shades will make them look smaller. Use a toning shadow or pencil for soft highlight up on the brow-bone. Remember that your eye make-up won't look good unless your brows are tidy and well-shaped, so pluck away stragglers from underneath for a really smooth finish.

down over the upper lashes and up under the lower lashes. Now finish off by brushing up under upper lashes and, down over lower lashes. Then, holding the brush sideways, draw it gently across the lashes so the little ones in the corners are coloured. This also helps to separate the lashes.

5. Lip Colour. If you haven't used a lip-brush before, now's the time to start. It's really simple . . . you'll soon get used to the idea and your lip colour will last much longer. Rest your elbow on something solid so your hand will be steady, then outline the shape of your lips carefully with the lip colour on the lip brush. Now fill in the rest with the colour on the brush.

These are the basic steps . . . you can experiment with all sorts of colours just as long as you stick to the rules. And remember that the whole idea is to make yourself look good, not disappear completely under layers and layers of thick make-up! Have fun making up — it's easy when you know how!

4. Mascara. It's pretty simple to apply really . . . the trick is to keep the lashes separated and to colour them *all*, even the little ones in the corners. Make sure your mascara brush isn't clogged

jackie Fashion PINNY~WISE

1. Rose-pink round necked pinafore with gingham trim. Catalogue No.: 6S678. Price: £7.99. Fabric: Cotton. Colours: Pink only. Sizes: 10 to 14.
Cream T-bar shoe with cream wedge. Style No.: A55/5534/80. Price: £8.99. Fabric: Leather. Colours: Cream, navy. Sizes: 3 to 8.

2. Round-necked denim pinafore with gingham trim. Price: £9.95. Fabric: Cotton. Colours: Blue only. Sizes: 10 to 14. Denim espadrille with woven look wedge. Style No.: 73/53052. Price: £3.99. Fabric: Denim. Colours: Blue, beige, green. Sizes: 3 to 7.

3. Super tiered wine pinafore with fine straps. Style No.: MD718. Price: £10.50. Fabric: Cotton. Colours: Wine only. Sizes: Small, medium, large.
Cream suede wedge shoe. Style No.: A10/56603. Price: £8.99. Fabric: Suede with leather wedge. Colours: Cream. Sizes: 3 to 8.

4. Blue floral print pinafore with criss-cross front and frilled hem. Style No.: 83220007. Price: £4.99. Fabric: Cotton. Colours: Assorted. Sizes: 10 to 16.
Brown sandal with wooden wedge and crepe sole. Price: £8.99. Fabric: Leather. Colours: Brown, black. Sizes: 3 to 7.

Pinafores are this Summer's big fashion extra! They make a fantastic contribution to your wardrobe because they're so versatile — wear them with shirts, jumpers or fine polos underneath, or by themselves when the sun shines extra hard. A pinafore is the one thing you just can't do without!

5. Bright red pinafore with criss-cross front and ties at the back. Style No.: 83000005. Price: £3.99. Fabric: Acrylic. Colours: Assorted. Sizes: 10 to 16. Open-toed beige T-bar sandal with square-backed wedge. Style: Geena. Price: £6.99. Fabric: Leather. Colours: Beige, brown, black. Sizes: 3 to 7.

6. Denim pinafore with patchwork pockets and unusual bib front. Style No.: 6524. Price: Approx. £10.95. Fabric: Cotton. Colours: Light blue, dark blue. Sizes: 10 to 14.
Cream suede shoe with star detail on front. Style No.: A11/56656. Fabric: Suede. Colours: Cream, tan. Sizes: 3 to 8.

7. Versatile round necked denim pinafore with toggle button trim. Style No.: AF202/6. Price: £5.99. Fabric: Denim. Colours: Blue only. Sizes: 12 to 16.
Denim sandal with floral embroidery and woven raffia wedge. Style No.: A15/25952. Price: £10.99. Fabric: Canvas. Colours: Blue, beige, black. Sizes: 3 to 8.

8. Colourful red/black/green floral print V-neck pinafore with ties at the back. Style No.: 2222. Price: £10.99. Fabric: Cotton rayon. Colours: Assorted. Sizes: 10 to 14. Delicate canvas sandal with plaited front and woven wedge. Style No.: A15/45535. Price: £5.99. Fabric: Canvas. Colours: Olive green, navy, beige. Sizes: 3 to 8.

Get into the stunning colour con
contrasts around.
Red means excitement and fu
for an explosive effect!

1. Red and black striped long sleeved dress with a black semi-circle design, from Jon Adam. Price: £25. Sizes: 10-14.
Black wooden beads and bangle, from Salisburys. Price: Beads, 80p; bangle, 60p.
Red peep-toe courts with a black flash design on uppers, from Sacha. Price: £29.99. Sizes: 3-7.

2. Black long sleeved jumper with red geometric design, from Top Shop. Price: £10.99. Sizes: 10-12.
Tapered black cord trousers with large front pockets, from Studio R. Price: £17.95. Sizes: 10-14.
Red ponytail clasp, from Baggage & General. Price: 65p.
Red wooden beads and bangle, from Salisburys. As for 1.
Black moccasin loafers with white uppers and tassles, from Ravel. Price: £18.99. Sizes: 3-7.

3. Red and black chessboard checked sleeveless mini dress, with high collar, from a selection at Snob.
Price: £18.99 approx. Sizes: 10-14.
Red button earrings, from Baggage & General. Price: 65p.
Red and black hexagonal bangles, from Baggage & General. Price: 75p each.
Black low-heeled stilettos with star punching detail, from Saxone. Price: £15.99. Sizes: 3-8.

4. Black knitted kne
glitter embroidery
Harold Ingram. Price
1 and 2.
Black hairband, fron
Price: 65p.
Red metallic bauble
& General. Price: 99
Red low-heeled cou
star punching detail
Price: £16.99. Sizes

MA
CONT

of black and red, one of the most dramatic
means mystery and intrigue — try both

...ress with red
...ulders, from
...approx. Sizes:

...e & General.

...rom Baggage

...eep toes and
...nfield.

...KE
...A
...RAST

5. Red V-necked T-shirt dress with side
slits, from the Body Shop. Price: £14.95.
Sizes: Small, medium, large.
Red metallic coral-style necklace, from
Baggage & General. Price: £1.99.
Black ponytail clasp, from Baggage &
General. As for 2.
Red basket weave high heeled mules, from
Ravel. Price: £16.99. Sizes: 3-7.

6. Black Aertex-style sweatshirt with red piping, from Simon
at Top Shop. Price: £8.99. Sizes:
10-14.
Red canvas straight skirt with
button-down slit pockets, from
Rebs. Price: £10.99. Sizes:
10-14.
Red hairband, from Baggage &
General. As for 4.
Red and black bangles, from
Baggage & General. Price: 75p
each.
Black ''College'' loafers with
tassles, from Saxone. Price:
£15.99. Sizes: 3-8.

7. Black long sleeved T-shirt, from
Top Shop. Price: £2.99. Sizes:
10-14.
Large red button earrings, from
Baggage & General. Price: 65p.
Red bauble and disc necklace, from
Baggage & General. Price: £1.99.
Black satin lizard-look tapered
trousers with red tie waistband, from
the Body Shop. Price: £25. Sizes:
10-14.
Red cutaway sling-back courts,
from Dolcis. Price: £14.99. Sizes:
3-8.

8. Red fitted jacket with black Chinese print,
and matching tapered trousers with tie waistband, from the Body Shop. Price: Jacket,
£19.95; trousers, £16.95. Sizes: Small, medium,
large.
Black liquorice stick necklace, from Baggage
& General. Price: £2.50 approx.
Red mules with conical heels and rosette
uppers, from Ravel. Price: £16.99. Sizes: 3-7.

Beauty Box

You can't fail to win him over with this special Valentine face, created specially for *Jackie* by make-up artist Celia Hunter. Read on and find out how to make it work for you!

WIN HIS HEART!

For a special Valentine date or disco, you need a special look, and that's what we've created here for model Caroline, just for you to copy. This is the special sultry look he won't be able to resist, and with just a little bit of practice, it's easy to perfect. Although we've specified techniques here, we haven't specified products, so you can make yourself up to look stunning our way, but using your own favourite products and shades, and matching colours to suit what you're wearing. Follow our step-by-step instructions for a look that will win you more than just admiring glances!

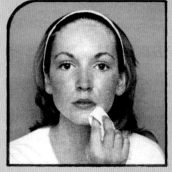

1. First, Celia cleansed Caroline's face with a creamy cleanser. After tissuing off and closing pores with toner, Celia smoothed in moisturiser, to keep skin soft and provide a base for foundation.

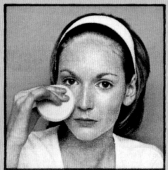

2. Always apply foundation cream with a damp cosmetic sponge. Celia also patted on translucent powder over shiny areas such as chin, nose and forehead, and also on eyelids to prevent eye make-up from creasing.

3. Celia used a powder blusher applied with a large, soft, natural bristle brush, and blended in carefully just under cheekbones. Choose either a pink or tawny-based shade to suit your skin tones and colouring.

4. To define eyes, apply eye pencil in a dark shade under lower lashes, and also to the eye socket, and blend.

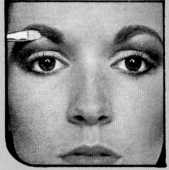

5. Celia then applied frosted mauve shadow to eyelids, and under the eyebrow. You may prefer cream or powder shadow, but remember always to use a brush or sponge applicator for a really even finish.

6. Mascara both top and lower eye lashes, and wait a few minutes for the first coat to dry before applying a second coat. Use a magnifying mirror while putting on mascara, and wipe away any smudges with the dampened tip of a cotton wool bud.

7. Apply lipstick carefully with a very slim lip brush, and add a touch of gloss for extra shine.

8. The finished look — hair softly curled for a super sexy effect!

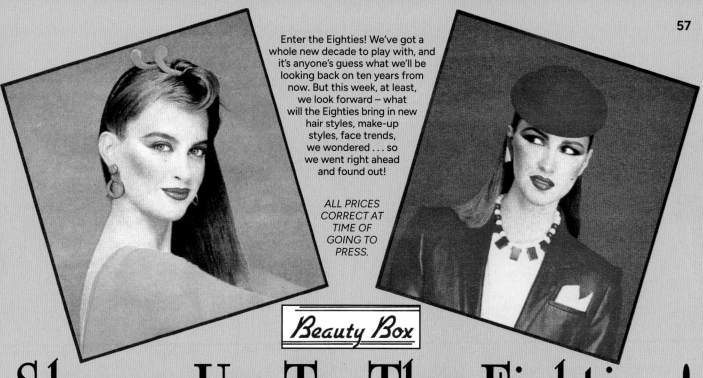

Enter the Eighties! We've got a whole new decade to play with, and it's anyone's guess what we'll be looking back on ten years from now. But this week, at least, we look forward – what will the Eighties bring in new hair styles, make-up styles, face trends, we wondered . . . so we went right ahead and found out!

ALL PRICES CORRECT AT TIME OF GOING TO PRESS.

Beauty Box

Shape Up To The Eighties!

SPRING-DRIVEN THING

Here, the geometric look has been taken through to spring by Mary Quant – her spring look incorporates bold, basic shades of turquoise and lilac, with a pinker shade for lips.

Eyeliner has been carefully applied here, and it's an art in itself, but one worth practising! Paint it just above lashes in a straight line curving slightly at the corners, just past the natural end of the lashes. Cake eye liner is the most economical – it'll literally last you for years. Eye liner defines and accentuates eye shape – an absolute must for eye appeal in the Eighties!

ON THE RIGHT LINES

Pencils are still big beauty news – and getting bigger. They're ideal for outlining, shaping, shading and blending, and must be about the most useful single item you can carry in your make-up bag.

Here, Miners have created this total fashion look, using only pencils, to complement the current geometric look. They've used four basic types of pencil – Miners Kohline, as the name suggests, is a soft, smudgy pencil, just right for defining eyes, slanting them outwards, and also for using as a dark shadow. In shades like black, brown, navy and grey, they cost 59p each.

Miners Eyebrow Pencils help to give you beautiful Liz Taylor-style eyebrows (but more about that later). These cost 34p, and come in black, browny-black, and browny-grey.

For well-defined lips, and for use as blusher and face shaper too, there's Miner's Lip Colour pencils. These are soft and slightly pearly, with shades like Shrimp, Scampi and Pepperoni for pink, Sixties-style lips, and Bully Brown for darker lips, price 45p.

Finally, eye colours – Miners Soft Eye Sticks, six fantastic soft pencils in black, blue, grey, white, turquoise and brown. Blend carefully for lid colour, or use as kohl pencils for a shiny evening look. Price 41p.

HAIR TODAY . . .

Eyebrows spent most of the Seventies being plucked out of sight, and occasionally being shaved off altogether. But the last year has seen them much more in evidence, and thick, more shaped eyebrows are a must for the vibrant, more stated make-up look that's with us now.

Growing in eyebrows is a rather labrious process, rather like growing out a short hair style, and you still need to keep plucking – for thick, don't fall into the trap of reading shapeless, too! It's worth persevering there, though, as thick eyebrows flatter most eye shapes, and you can help them along by pencilling in short, fine lines, in a shade nearest to your own colouring.

IF YOU WANT TO GET AHEAD . . .

. . . get a hair-cut – we show you some of the latest styles below.

1. New "High-Tech" style from the Ginger Group Academy. This is a graduated cut, short and sleek at the back, going into a 'V' at the ears, but leaving fullness at the front to add softness.

2. Full Of Body – a style from Irvine Rusk of Scotland, with Clynol's Uniperm.

3. Hair by Remy of Remy at Leicester – the asymmetric movement is with Clynol's new perm, Waves.

4. Not the most practical of styles, perhaps, but bound to get you noticed – "Halo" by Jingles, coloured with Clynol's Vitonesse permanent creme-tint.

YOU'RE STILL IN THE SEVENTIES IF . . .

. . . you're still not considering anything other than another frizzy perm for your hair
. . . your lips are still running over with greasy lip gloss
. . . your eyebrows are so thin they can't be seen
. . . your only eye shadow is powder blue

. . . your nails are pearlised
. . . your hair's the same mousey brown it's been for years
. . . your only make-up shades are dull old browns and greys
. . . your only eye make-up is thick black kohl worn on the insides of eyes – nothing makes eyes look smaller!

SHAPE UP

Finally, we had a word with Berlei, famous for their surveys on shape, as well as their very good underwear and foundation garments, to see just how they see us shaping up in the Eighties.

Our shape is constantly changing, they told us; but any changes will be very, very slight. All indications point to us becoming marginally taller and slimmer with slightly less bust, and a thickening around the waist and hips, eventually leading to a shape that's very slightly more masculine.

Seventies make-up looks were very influenced by punk, and latterly, the return to the Sixties/mod look, a style that's still with us. We can tell you what's in as we go into the Eighties, but as for what they hold in future – that's quite another matter . . . !

There are lots of lovely, muted fruity colours around just now — mulberries, cranberries, damsons and dark plums. Mix any of these together, or add a splash of neutral grey and you'll look as delicious as the real thing!

JuIcy

1. Mulberry fluffy jacket with boa collar and zip pocket, from Misfits by Mo. Price: £29.50. Sizes: Small, medium, large.
Grey cords, from Razzy. Price: £16.50. Sizes: 26-34 in.
Burgundy padded ankle boots, from Dolcis. Price: £24.99. Sizes: 3-8.

2. Cranberry glazed padded jacket and matching tapered trousers, from the Warehouse. Price: Jacket, £16.99; trousers, £12.99. Sizes: 10-14.
Burgundy fringed loafers, from Dolcis. Price: £16.99. Sizes: 3-8.

3. Dark plum fluffy sweatshirt dress with side buttoning on collar, from Les Toupies. Price: £30. Sizes: 10-14.
Lilac scalloped shoulder bag, from Top Shop. Price: £7.99.
Pale grey ankle socks with lilac bobbles, from Jump at Palms. Price: £3.50. Sizes: One size.
Purple suede pumps with ankle strap and ties, from Medway. Price: £20. Sizes: 3-8.

4. Plum and burgundy multi-stripe rain jacket, from Alfie. Price: £26.50. Sizes: 10-14.
Damson fluffy sweatshirt with zip pocket, from Palms. Price: £10.90. Sizes: Small, medium, large.
Damson suede-look baggy tapered trousers, from Clarks. Price: £2?. Sizes: 10-14.
Dark violet pumps with punched uppers, from Dolcis. Price: £16.99. Sizes: 3-8.

fruits!

5. Cranberry crew-neck jumper with satin butterfly applique, from Peter Robinson. Price: £11.99. Sizes: Small, medium, large.
Damson and blue checked skirt with front pleat, from Dorothy Perkins. Price: £9.99. Sizes: 10-14.
Burgundy patent pumps with black piping, from Curtess. Price: £9.99. Sizes: 3-8.

6. Damson button-up jacket and matching ski pants, from Howie at Palms. Price: Jacket, £18.90; trousers, £12.50. Sizes: Small, medium, large.
Grey low-heeled stilettos with polka dot design, from Saxone. Price: £17.99. Sizes: 3-8.

7. Grey and plum striped sweatshirt, from Paul Simon. Price: £9.95. Sizes: Small, medium, large.
Grey scalloped shoulder bag, from Waves. Price: £7.99.
Cranberry corduroy straight skirt, from Rebs. Price: £10.99. Sizes: Small, medium, large.
Grey fringed loafers, from Clarks Neon range. Price: £17.99. Sizes: 3-7.

8. Mulberry loose-knit sweater, from Snob. Price: £17.99. Sizes: 10-14.
Mulberry and turquoise checked full skirt, from Alfie. Price: £10.99. Sizes: 10-14.
Pale grey fluffy gloves with ties, from Jump at Palms. Price: £3.99.
Burgundy lace-ups with lilac trim, from Trueform. Price: £13.99. Sizes: 3-8.

party!

Dance the night away in a stunning little number...

Black and tartan suit;
£32.99, from Chelsea Girl.
Tartan elasticated belt;
£8.99, from Flash Trash.
Red silk scarf, in hair; £2.99,
from Flash Trash.

Velvet fringed jacket;
£19.99, from Top Shop.
Pink taffeta skirt; £18.99,
from Top Shop.
Pink net skirt, worn
underneath; £16.99, from
Top Shop.
Pink teddy; £11.99, from
Chelsea Girl.
Purple and black earrings;
£2.99, from Flash Trash.

Red military-style dress with gold
buttons; £29.99, from Chelsea Girl.

party!

Black velvet stretch dress; £19.99, from Top Shop.

Mustard silk button-down jacket; £12.99, from Chelsea Girl.

Gold shimmer scarf; £2.99, from Flash Trash.

Orange beads; £1.99, from Flash Trash.

Chunky gold bangles; £2.99 each, from Chelsea Girl.

Heavy gold gate bracelet; £8.99, from Flash Trash.

Glitter drop diamond earrings; £4.99, from Flash Trash.

Green and black print strapless dress with black net underskirt; £29.99, from Top Shop.

Green shimmer scarf, in hair; £2.99, from Flash Trash.

Gold leaf hoop earrings; £1.75, from Chelsea Girl.

Gold flat choker necklace; £4.99, from Chelsea Girl.

Layer It

JACKIE FASHION

1. Purple boucle double breasted jacket, from Top Coat. Price: £35 approx. Sizes: 10-14.

2. Traditional denim jacket, from Clarks. Price: £19.50. Sizes: Small, medium, large.

3. Cream knitted jacket with Pink Panther applique, from Irvine Sellars. Price: £17.99. Sizes: 10-14.
   Lilac knitted hat with peak, from Sara Lou. Price: £3.99.

4. Blue satin-look tiger print quilted jacket, from Clothilde. Price: £39.95. Sizes: Small, medium, large.

5. Wild West design parka with hood, from Hoofer. Price: £19.95. Sizes: One size.

6. Pastel checked fleecy duffel jacket, from Misfits by Mo. Price: £40. Sizes: Small, medium, large.
   Mint green mittens with bobbles, from Sara Lou. Price: £2.50.

7. White satin-look quilted jacket, from Alfie. Price: £23.99. Sizes: 10-14.
   Cream patterned gloves, from Debenhams. Price: £1.50.

8. Grey blazer, from Top Coat. Price: £29.50 approx. Sizes: 10-14.
   Blue, grey and red striped college scarf, from Chelsea Girl. Price: £2.49.

9. Burgundy padded jacket with fleecy collar, from Chelsea Girl. Price: £16.95. Sizes: 10-14.

10. Lilac double breasted blazer, from Jaqui. Price: £32.95. Sizes: 10-14.
    Lilac patterned gloves, from Salisburys. Price: £2.99.

11. Navy rain jacket with drawstring waist, from Valstar. Price: £24 approx. Sizes: 10-14.
    Navy patterned gloves, from Chelsea Girl. Price: £1.65.

12. Cream, grey and grape striped padded jacket, from Chelsea Girl. Price: £19.95. Sizes: 1, 2, 3.
    Grape fluffy gloves and scarf, from Salisburys. Price: Gloves, £2.99; scarf, £3.99.

13. Grey zig-zag padded jacket with penguin applique on back, from Misfits by Mo. Price: £39.90. Sizes: Small, medium, large.

14. Lilac flecked double breasted blouson jacket, from Alfie. Price: £29. Sizes: 10-14.

15. Straight denim jacket with patch pockets. from F.U.'s. Price: £20. Sizes: 10-16.
    Red plastic mini duffel bag with blue fringing and beads, from Sara Lou. Price: £2.99.

16. Dark camouflage padded jacket, from Alfie. Price: £19.95. Sizes: 10-14.

On!

In many ways, a cosy jacket can be a better buy than a more expensive coat because it's more versatile.

Most of the jackets shown here will look equally good with dresses, skirts or trousers, but will give you plenty of protection from the elements, too!

WHITE MAGIC!

On dark mornings and evenings, make sure you're visible to one a
in the brightest of bright whites! Keep warm in white woollies, white
and white tweed and mix it with fur-lined boots for maximum warmt
energy!

All the cleverest animals change their coats to white for winter, so f
their lead and start at the top with a white woolly hat, add a big Aran ju
and cord skirt, thick white woolly tights, gloves and legwarmers. I
like, add subtle toning colours, like a grey fleck cardigan or sweatsh
something sparkly for evening with subtle Lurex threads!

You can wear it night or day and still look white and wonderful!

TUFTY TAILS

SARAH is 18 and a temporary secretary. He
Tony trimmed Sarah's hair before styling it. He
divided it into sections which he put into braids then
gelled and sprayed into place.

IT'S A STICK-UP!

JOANN is 20 and a civil servant.
Tony cut Joann's hair into this spiky style then
coloured the tips. It can be worn lots of different
ways — Joann can keep it spiky for a night out or
wear it flatter for work.

SNIPPING IMAGE

TRACEY is 19 and a student.
Tracey's hair was cut to show that short hair
needn't always look the same! To compliment the
dramatic hairstyle the make up is quite severe.

6

WHAT'S YOUR PROBLEM

OUR BEAUTY ED HAS THE ANSWERS . . .

I'm really fed-up with my hair and would like to change it completely. I've thought about getting it permed and coloured but is it possible to have both things done at the same time?

If your hair is in good condition then it is possible but most hairdressers recommend you wait at least a week after a perm before getting your hair coloured. (You should never perm hair which has recently been coloured.)

If you decide to go ahead then I strongly recommend you go to a professional hairdresser — don't attempt this at home! Ask your hairdresser's advice about after-care too and make sure you get your hair trimmed regularly afterwards to keep it in top condition.

I don't usually wear much make-up but I'd like to try using some foundation. The only problem is I don't have a clue where to start!

Well, the first decision you'll have to make is what foundation you should buy. For young skins a light foundation is all that's needed and try to choose one in a shade as near as possible to your natural skin colouring. Dot it over your face and neck and blend in well either with clean fingertips or, for a more professional finish, a damp cosmetic sponge. Remember to take it right up to your hairline and under your jawline to avoid any harsh edges. Finally, finish off with a light dusting of translucent face powder.

My eyelashes are really pale but if I apply a few coats of mascara they seem to go brittle and get clogged up. Any suggestions?

Firstly take a look at your mascara. If it contains fibres then this could be what's causing the 'clogged' effect. Choose a mascara without fibres or, alternatively, have your eyelashes dyed. You can get this done professionally at most beauticians or buy a kit and do it yourself at home. This usually lasts for around six weeks and means you won't have to apply mascara every day.

I plucked my eyebrows recently and got a bit carried away so there isn't much left of them. Is there anything I can do to make them grow in quicker?

Unfortunately, I'm afraid not. Eyebrows are really best left as natural as possible by just plucking stragglers from below the browbone and across the bridge of the nose. The only thing I can suggest is you buy an eyebrow pencil as close to your natural hair colour as possible and pencil in a few 'false' hairs. Don't go overboard though or they'll just look worse!

Can you tell me how to use eyelash curlers and will they hurt?

Eyelash curlers are useful contraptions which may look a bit scary but, if used properly, shouldn't hurt at all! Just hold them open over your top eyelashes then squeeze down firmly but gently and tilt your hand upwards whilst doing so. Hold for a few seconds then release. You should now have curly lashes! (Always use the eyelash curlers before applying mascara or you could damage your lashes.)

My boyfriend and I are planning to get engaged soon and I'm really looking forward to showing off the ring but my hands and nails are a mess. Any suggestions?

It might be worth investing in a visit to your local beautician for a professional manicure. This should only cost a few pounds and will get your hands and nails in good shape so that you can then begin to take good care of them properly. It's probably best to have all your nails trimmed to the same length so you can start from scratch. Use a good hand cream regularly (choose one which conditions nails too) and always wear good rubber gloves when washing clothes, doing dishes, etc.

I tend to get quite a few spots but my cheeks are very dry and flaky. Can you tell me the best way to look after my skin?

It sounds as if you could have combination skin which is a mixture of dry and oily areas. Usually the skin around the eyes, cheeks and neck is dry and the forehead, nose and chin are slightly oily. The best way to treat this type of skin is to use products specially formulated for each area.

To help prevent those spots stick to a healthy diet with lots of fruit and veg and cleanse your skin thoroughly morning and night.

the best

...e gave six Jackie readers a
...vetty twendy make-over ...

BLEACH BOY
And now for something completely different!
BONNY'S dark skinhead was shaved even
shorter and bleached blond. Who's a pretty boy
then?!

FRINGE BENEFIT
CLAIRE is 18 and a hairdresser.
Tony has layered Claire's long hair to give it
fullness without losing any of the length.

BOBBING ALONG
Matt styled Liz's hair to show that a bob is for
... from bonny!

Liz is cool a hairdresser.

Hair by TONY ALLEN,
30 Alexandra Street, Southend-On-Sea, Essex.
Make-up by Claire Broderick.

...ING FOR A ...NGE!

...ays it's possible to change
...ir of your hair almost as
...ou change the colour of your
... You can spray on colour
... Streaks 'n' Tips or Boots
...ightning colour sprays;
...se temporary colourants
...until you next wash your
... Innecto's Hint of a Tint
...s and Toners; or semi-
... colourants that last
... shampoos like Glints and
...r for a complete change.
...e a permanent colour
...ast until your hair grows
... choice!

...enough the whole hair
...iness began at least
... ago when the Kings
...abylon are said to have
...ust to colour their hair!
... used to cover their
...ith tea infusions while
...en used to bleach their
...ipes based on quick-
...ood ash mixed with

...choice is yours — but
...ssional advice if you
...g the colour of your
...tly and dramatically,
... end up wanting to
...out!

THE BIG CLEAN UP!

Now's the time to clean up your beauty routine! Invest in a jumbo-size tube of Anne French Deep Cleansing Cream (£1.29), then use it to clean away the day's dirt and make-up in the following way.

Squeeze some cream into the palm of your hand; this'll warm it slightly so it sinks into your skin more easily. With the fingers of your other hand gently dot it all over your face and neck and massage it into your skin as lightly as possible. Always start from the neck and work upwards to counteract the natural tendency of the face muscles to droop. Sweep up the neck then with the first two fingers of each hand work up along the jawline from chin to ears. Then, again using the first two fingers of each hand, work up and along the cheekbones. Stroke round and over the mouth, and massage up to your forehead from the bridge of the nose to the hairline. Then gently cleanse around the eye area using light, circular massaging movements. Wipe away the cream and the day's grime with it with cotton wool or a tissue. Then splash your face with cold water to tone your skin and help close the pores.

STAR ...UALITY!

...ey Lewis lets us into
...e of her beauty
...s ...

...ws has come a long way since performing
... for the likes of George Michael. She's released
... 'You Used To Be) Romantic' and she's
...friendly' with a certain member of Bros.
...s Shirley's secret for success? We asked a
...tions to find out ...

...SE
...my skin as clear as possible by using a good
...aking sure I never go to bed with make-up
...'t usually suffer from spots so I don't need a
...I usually just apply a light dusting of
...owder to even out my skin tone.

...SPECIAL
...anywhere special I like to give my skin a
...Normally I just wear some eyeshadow and
...Rubenstein liquid eyeliner.

SPECIAL
...sessions and personal appearances I
...ke-up so my face doesn't look too shiny
... I usually apply blusher, too, to give my
...finition.

LIPSMACKIN'
"I always carry a lipstick in my pocket for emergencies — it's amazing how much difference it can make. I usually go for fairly light shades for a pale but interesting pout!"

CURL UP 'N' DYE
"I use a jet black dye and a spiral perm to pep up my naturally dark brown hair. For appearances on stage I sometimes add a few extensions to give extra body. To keep them looking natural I wash and condition them every day just like normal hair!"

FIGHTING FIT
"When I'm on tour I usually take my exercise machine with me. It's light and easy to carry but, best of all, it helps keep me in shape. I love chips but I've been trying to stick to one proper meal a day, usually fish, and lots of non-fattening grapefruit juice!"

ALL CHANGE
"Bros recommended that old favourite American Classics so I popped down and found myself a new image — Doc Marten boots, ripped jeans and some dead cool leather jackets too!"

STYLE IT YOURSELF!

It's never too early to spring into spring, especially if the winter woes are starting to get you down in a big way! And even if you're still suffering from a post-Christmas cash crisis, there is a way to brighten up your life and make the warm weather days come that little bit closer.

Fill up the dark nights by making yourself a whole new spring and summer wardrobe with the help of Style patterns. The three shown here are only a taste of the great selection of ideas they've come up with so that you can look good! The patterns cost from around £1.35 to £1.95 at most large department stores and there are lots of different styles and details to choose from.

Don't waste your winter evenings mooning around, waiting for something to happen – get your needle out and get stuck into a whole new summer look!

JACKIE FASHION

BE HIS

1. Pink sleeveless dress with fan embroidery, lilac piping and tie belt, from Clothilde. Price: £22.99 approx. Sizes: 10-14. Flower hair-comb, from Corocraft. Price: £1.50. Enamelled flower necklet, from Corocraft. Price: £1.50. Pink and silver metallic bangles, from Baggage & General. Price: Approx. 65p each. Flat pink pumps with star punch detail around upper, from Ravel. Price: £15.99. Sizes: 3-7.

2. Black strapless boned dress with tulip side slit and bow, and matching edge to edge jacket with belt, from Mushroom. Price: £30 approx. Sizes: 10-14. Dark blue enamelled teardrop earrings, from Tailpieces. Price: £3.45 approx. Pink enamelled butterfly necklet, from Corocraft. Price: £2.50. Pink sheer tights, from Omsa. Price: 79p. Dark blue low courts with peep-toe and star punch detail, from Manfield. Price: £16.99. Sizes: 3-8.

3. Black V-necked dress with gold shell embroidery on shoulders, and gold belt, from Greek Connection. Price: £18.50. Sizes: 10-14. Gold-look lover's knot necklet, from Corocraft. Price: £2.25. Black patent strappy sandals, from Dolcis. Price: £13.99. Sizes: 3-8.

4. Black heart print dress with three-quarter-length sleeves and sweetheart neckline, from Mr Ant at Timbuc 2. Price: £35.95 approx. Sizes: 10-16. Pink enamelled flower earrings, from Corocraft. Price: £2.95. Treble rope of pearls, from Corocraft. Price: £1.65. Deep pink scallop-edged leather clutch bag, from Ravel. Price: £15.99. Bright blue sheer tights, by Omsa. Price: 79p. Deep pink low wedge, peep toe sandals with ankle strap and white piping, from Ravel. Price: £14.99. Sizes: 3-7.

HEART-THROB !

5. Yellow embossed, slinky, high-necked dress, with back slit and tapered sleeves, from The Warehouse. Price: £21.99. Sizes: 10-14. Large black hair-comb, from Tailpieces. Price: Approx. 95p. Black and white conical droplet earrings, from Tailpieces. Price: £2.95. Black high-heeled courts, from Dolcis. Price: £12.99. Sizes: 3-8.

6. Black and red patterned slinky dress with ruched front and tie straps, from Greek Connection. Price: £18.50. Sizes: 10-14. Red metallic beads, from Baggage & General. Price: From 65p. Red lattice work mules, from Ravel. Price: £15.99. Sizes: 3-7.

7. Purple patterned see-through long shirt top and matching purple crepe trousers, from Top Shop. Price: £44.99. Sizes: 10-14. Purple lightning clip-on earrings, from Corocraft. Price: £2.95. Purple heart-shaped velvet bag, from Top Shop. Price: £6.25 Purple low-heeled courts with punch detailed uppers, from Dolcis. Price: £15.99. Sizes: 3-8.

8. Blue print seersucker sundress with rick-rack braiding and sweetheart neckline, from Mr Ant at Timbuc 2. Price: £25 approx. Sizes: 8-14. Blue enamelled heart necklet, from Corocraft. Price: £2.50. White canvas flatties with black piping and strap, from Ravel. Price: £7.99. Sizes: 3-7.

Well-Plaid!

Mix tartans and checks for a fun, confused muddle of colour . . . and explain that you've simply got your lines crossed!

1

2

3

4

5

BLACK CURRENTS!

Take bla
with bloc
a mudd
hues or a

Jackie Fashion

Every page in "Jackie" was made with love and creativity — and you could tell. The magazine was always at the cutting edge of design. From the layouts and the lighting, to the models and the clothes, each issue looked stunning.

2.

1.

1.
Jacket by
Borderline,
from a
range at Top
Shop, Oxford
Circus.
Shirt, £20.30.
From Stefanel.
Skirt, £8.99.
From Chelsea
Girl.
Hockey boots,
£7.99. From
selected sports
shops.
Sunspecs,
model's own.

2.
Jacket, £19.99.
From a Freemans agent
or direct from
Sue Snowdon,
139 Clapham Road,
London SW9.
State catalogue
no. (KO6100),
size required,
and enclose a
cheque or
postal order.
Shirt by Aitch,
£12.99. From
Chelsea Man.
Skirt, £7.99.
From Chelsea Girl.
Earrings, model's own.

Shirt by Je
Rogers, £
From Top
and S
Skirt, £1
approx. £
Top S
Shoes, £1
(plus £
p. and p.), F
Shelly's Sh
159 Ox
Street, Lon

Splat!

KAREN SEDDON

STELLA CARR

TIM ROME

TIM ROME

MARK PARKER

KAREN SEDDON

Make-up by Carrie.

1. Black and white dogtooth suit, £27.95. Sizes: 10-14. One colour only. Available from a Freemans agent (catalogue No. WK6505) or direct from Sue Snowdon, 139 Clapham Road, London SW9. Red tights by Dim, £1.95 approx. Available from department stores. White shoes, £17.99. Sizes: 3-8. Colours: Assorted. Available from branches of Manfield.

2. Green T-shirt from Pinto, £2.99. Sizes: S, M, L. Colours: Assorted. Available from Pinto, 125 King's Road, London SW3. Black and blue checked shirt from Pinto. M, L. Colours: Assorted. Available... black checked trousers, £15.99. Sizes: 10-14. Colours: Assorted. Available from Chelsea Girl.

...and white checked shirt from Pinto, £14.99. Sizes: S, M, L. One colour only. ...before.
...skirt also from Pinto, £14.99. Sizes: S, M, L. One colour only. Available from major department stores.
...red beads by Adrien Mann, £5.95 approx. Available from major department stores.

...T-shirt from Pinto, details as before. Sizes: S, M, L. Colours: Assorted. Available from ...ted skirt by Jeffrey Rogers, £13.99. Sizes: S, M, L. Colours: Assorted. Available from branches of Top Shop, Miss Selfridge, Chelsea Girl and Fenwicks of Brent Cross. ...glan-sleeved coat with checked lining, £34.99. Sizes: S, M, L. One colour only. Available branches of Dorothy Perkins.

...ck shirt, £3.99 approx. From a wide selection available from Flip at Long Acre, London ...urtain Road, London EC4; King's Road, London SW3. One colour only. Stockist as before. ...h jacket from Pinto, £29.95. Sizes: S, M, L. Colours: Assorted. Available from branches of ...users, £21.99. Sizes: S, M, L. ...ed. Available from branches of Saxone and Lilley &

...sic and bring it to life
...our — whether it's
...of shades and
...park of red.

5. Cardigan, £19.99, catalogue no. KX1516. From Freemans. details as for 2. Shirt from Stefanel as before. Skirt by Jelly Designs, £15.99 approx. From Top Shop, Oxford Circus. Hockey boots, details as before.

6. Sweater from a range at Top Shop and Dorothy Perkins. Skirt, £10.99. From Top Shop. Shirt from Stefanel as before.

...ly gals everywhere are
...— and Michael Graber
...olour too. Their range of
...ain's best young artists.
...ar it on your back?
...t Koko, Covent Garden;
...arrods; and at selected
...down the t-shirts, write
...W2.

4. Jacket from a range at Top Shop and Dorothy Perkins. Shirt by Jeffrey Rogers, £12.99. From Harrods and James Beattie in the Midlands. Skirt by Borderline, £15.99 approx. From Top Shop, Oxford Circus. Socks, £1.49. From Flip. Bag from a range at Flip.

Seeing *Stars*

No. 815 AUGUST 18, 1979   THURSDAYS   9p

Jackie
NUMBER ONE FOR FUN!

WHO'LL BE YOUR HOLIDAY HUNK? Find Out On page

NEW! STARTS TODAY! Dramatic Photo Feature! WHAT'S YOUR PROBLEM?

TASTY JAM PIN-UP

J ACKIE was not only the magazine for girls to be seen holding; it was also the place to be for celebrities on the rise. For one much-loved actress, the pages of "Jackie" were to provide a magical introduction to being in the public eye. Lesley Ash, star of "Quadrophenia" and sit-com "Men Behaving Badly", was a regular model in the fashion and beauty pages of "Jackie", and graced the cover on several occasions. With her fresh face and shiny, long hair, Lesley was the ideal "canvas" for a long list of stylists and beauticians who were keen to share their expertise in the magazine's pages. And with her frequent appearances on the front page, smiling brightly on the newsstands, it can be argued that Lesley is the quintessential "Jackie" girl!

ARE YOU A FLOP?

BEAUTY BOX

Feel your hair's a complete flop? If *your* hair's always a mess, you'll know what we mean! Tatty hair ruins your whole image, no matter how much care you take with your clothes and make-up, so take steps now to make your hair into your crowning glory. It's simple enough, so hair goes . . .

I F you're as fed up as Lesley in our photo, you'll need to take instant action! Her hair's naturally wavy and a good colour, but right now she looks like most of us feel from time to time . . . fed up!

We rushed Lesley along to top stylist Sue at the Elida Gibbs salon in London to ask her advice. Sue diagnosed the problem at once!

"Like lots of girls, Lesley's hair is inclined to be greasy and that often makes it hard to manage," she told us. "And not being cut in a definite style makes it look a bit frayed around the edges when it needs a wash.

"Anyone with greasy hair should use a mild shampoo for washing, one that helps to remove excess grease without disturbing the natural balance of basic oils which are necessary for keeping the hair healthy!

"It's important to wash gently, making sure that scalp and hair are clean and rinsing very thoroughly. The water should be warm, not hot."

While Sue was telling us this, Lesley's hair was being washed with Pears Shampoo for greasy hair, and she emerged with it wet and ready for trimming. Lesley shrank at the sight of the scissors, but Sue was very firm.

"The secret of a really successful hairstyle is a good, basic cut," she says, "only professional cutting will ensure that your hair looks good all the time. A trim once a month will get rid of split and damaged ends and keep the shape right."

After a thorough wash with a mild shampoo like Pears Shampoo for greasy hair, the hair's rinsed really well and cutting begins.

SOFT AND SHINY

Blow-drying's a quick, simple way of keeping your hair natural and beautiful. All you need's a good cut, a drier and a circular brush!

Success. A glossy, smooth style that's right for anytime. And you really can do it yourself at home, once you've been for the basic cut!

Blow-drying's best for easy, natural styles, and it's a very simple way of keeping hair nice, once you've got the basic style! All you need is a drier and a *round* brush for styling and shaping as you dry.

Sue showed Lesley how to blow-dry her hair herself after it had been trimmed and shaped, and gave us a few hints on blow-drying at home.

...too close to the look. Don't use steel combs or spiky, wiry brushes either, as these can strip the outer layers of hair, leaving it in very bad condition."

Lesley's finished straight style was neatly turned under and very smooth and shiny, shaped down the sides to give an angular line. Sue stressed that the hair *must* be clean and shining for this style to look its best. And Lesley certainly looks at her very best now!

TOP TIPS

Your hair won't look right unless the basic cut is good. So don't moan if your hair looks terrible, go to a hairdresser and have something done about it!

Do use a shampoo that's right for your hair-type and do choose a mild shampoo if you have greasy hair. Pears Shampoo for greasy hair costs 29p, 44p or 75p for the economy size.

Always treat your hair gently—tugging with spiky brushes and combs will damage the hair and cause split ends.

Don't despair if your hair isn't in good condition, though. With correct cutting and conditioning it will be shining and healthy in just a few months!

ADD A BIT OF BOUNCE

...ecial occasions.
...set the hair
...up at the back

It's easy to get bored with a style, though, so we asked Sue to give Lesley a softer, curlier look for special occasions.

She used heated rollers for the evening style, showing Lesley how she can do exactly the same thing herself at home. The rollers are set back over the top and sides of the head, with the

bottom hair rolled up at the back.

If you don't have heated rollers, you can achieve the same effect with ordinary rollers, setting the hair while it's still wet.

The final result's smooth on top, curly and bouncy at the sides ... just right for any special occasion!

Great for evening ... this style ... but very simple to do yourself ... heated or ordinary rollers.

Famous *Faces*

Eeek. You're *not* going out in that dress. . . are you?

FRIGHT FROCKS

2. Yellow print frock, £5.00; yellow cardie, 75p; scarf in hair. 50p.

1 & 3 Green 1950's frock, £2.50; scarf in hair, 50p; Victorian glass beads, £5.50; basket, £1.50; Doc Marten shoes, model's own. Toys, fashion Ed's own.

5. Black velvet 1940's frock, £10.00; black beret, £1.50; leather briefcase, £2.50; diamante poodle-brooch (on beret) £1.50.

4. Black and white frock, £4.00; Grey 1960's cardie, £4.50; white gloves, £1.25.

If you're a sucker for little-girl frocks and dear woolly cardies like mummy used to knit, you probably know by now that they're not that easy to come by. Not since you grew too tall for Mothercare, anyhow . . .

Good hunting grounds for those who fear jumble sales as much as the ladies department in Marks and Sparks are the 2nd hand fashion shops springing up far and wide where the frocks are all nice and clean and good as new. Some of the stock actually is unworn, and it's a lot cheaper than chainstore fashion, too . . . Check out your local cities for a helping of retro style.

ABERDEEN: Relax, 116 Rosemount Viaduct.
BATH: Loose Threads, 1 Grove St.
BELFAST: American Madness, Howard St.
BIRMINGHAM: Mega-Active, 113-133 Corporation St.
BRISTOL: Paradise Garage, 3a Haymarket Walk.
CARDIFF: Antique Market, The Hayes.
DUBLIN: Xanadu, 19 Drury Street.
GLASGOW: Flip, Queens Street.
LEEDS: Other Clothes, 10 Empire Arcade.
LIVERPOOL: 69A, 69A Renshaw St.
LONDON: Flip, 26 Long Acre.
NEWCASTLE: The Attic, 9a The Haymarket.
NOTTINGHAM: Gladrags & Backstage, 9 Clinton Street West.
PLYMOUTH: Upstairs, Downstairs, 1 Camden St., Devonshire St.
SHEFFIELD: Mussons, 75 Carvel Street.
YORK: Antique Market, 2 Lendal.

All clothes from a selection of styles at retro fashion shops throughout the country.

BEING SMALL, I ALWAYS LOOK FOR CLOTHES WHICH MAKE ME LOOK A BIT TALLER," TOYAH TOLD US.

"FOR INSTANCE, I'D NEVER CHOOSE ANYTHING WITH HORIZONTAL STRIPES WHICH WOULD MAKE ME LOOK FATTER THAN I AM!

"Smaller people do have a problem when it comes to buying clothes and I have to be very careful to make sure that I go for darker colours, which tend to be more flattering."

Toyah likes to shop for her clothes in unusual, back-street shops.

"I prefer the not so well-known shops because I don't want to go somewhere and find someone else in exactly the same outfit," she told us.

Toyah is very interested in fashion and feels that it's very, very important.

"What you wear should reflect your own personal taste. I don't always believe in being told what to wear!

"Clothes are a very big part of your individuality. You should feel good in what you wear. Above all, though, your clothes should be comfortable."

Toyah spends a lot of money on clothes now, particularly on her stage clothes, but she wasn't always in this position.

"When I was a drama student I couldn't afford many new clothes, but I still really cared about what I dressed in.

"I got all my clothes from places like jumble sales and the wardrobe department of the theatre!

"If you don't have much m...

SHIRLEY MANSON

BUCKS FIZZ

OVER the decades, the fashion and beauty pages of "Jackie" magazine became legendary for featuring those who were on the cusp of superstardom.

It was no "mystery" why singing sensation Toyah Wilcox was storming up the charts – her distinctive voice and appearance made her a natural performer.

However she was even more well-known to the readers of "Jackie", who had already seen her model some exciting trends over the years.

Likewise, alt-rocker Shirley Manson of Garbage fame also cut her teeth in front of the camera showing off some truly eye-catching dresses.

Bucks Fizz, meanwhile, always looked the very glamorous part!

JACKIE FASHION

We've all admired actress/singer TOYAH WILLCOX on screen and stage, so now's your chance to see her in a different light — as a model for our fashion pages! Toyah picked out all the clothes herself, using her own individual style to put them all together. Which, for Toyah, is just doing what comes naturally!

on clothes, I think it's important to buy one outfit that you really like, and wear it all the time — rather than buying lots of accessories and things.

"When I was a drama student I used to go around in this long black coat and a pair of heavy black platform shoes — I loved the outfit and wore it all the time!"

TOYAH FEELS THAT HER CLOTHES ARE A VERY IMPORTANT PART OF HER IMAGE. SHE'S WELL KNOWN FOR APPEARING IN SOME STUNNING STAGE OUTFITS, BUT WOULD HATE TO BE PREDICTABLE, WHICH IS WHY SHE LIKES USING YOUNG, NEW DESIGNERS.

Whereas before, she didn't feel that accessories were important if you haven't got a lot of money to spend on clothes, Toyah feels that the jewellery she wears on stage is an essential part of her look.

"On stage, the accessories are just as important as the outfit."

Judging by the selection that Toyah brought along to our photographic session, her own accessories are as individual and dramatic as the girl herself!

Finally, we asked her if there was anyone she admired for their clothes sense.

"James Dean and David Bowie. Bowie always looks so fantastic. Whereas so many of

TOYAH WILCOX

Bucks Fizz show you some of the brightest, bubbliest clothes around. If you want to grab a piece of the action, clothes like these are bound to add a touch of sparkle to anything you do!

FIZZING FASHION!

JACKIE FASHION

Hair by Rocky.
Make-up by Audrey Maxwell.

CHERYL wears: Orange and gold sparkling net ballgown from Liberated Lady. Price: £29.95. Sizes: 8-14. Colours: Black, white. Jewellery by Adrien Mann. Shoes — Cheryl's own.

JAY wears: Gold/black Lurex body stocking from Liberated Lady. Price: £7. Sizes: One size only. Colours: Silver, black and other assorted colours. Bright red tiered mini skirt from Hindukush. Price: £15. Sizes: Small, medium, large. Colours: Assorted fabrics and colours. From Hindukush, 231 Portobello Road, London SW11. Readers' enquiries to above.

CHERYL wears: Red/gold puff-sleeved dress (worn as top) with full tiered skirt to match from Liberated Lady. Price: £29.95. Matching full tiered skirt from Liberated Lady. Price: £15.95. Sizes: Small, medium, large. Colours: Red, purple, black. Shoes — Cheryl's own.

LIBERATED LADY clothes are available from Liberated Lady, 406 King's Road, London SW3. A mail order list is available from the above address (enclose an s.a.e.). Items featured on this page are available by post from the above address. (Add £1 to cover postage and packing.)

JAY wears: Orange satin "balloon shorts" with gold detail and matching jacket from Liberated Lady. Price: £29.95. Sizes: 8-14. Colours: White, black, orange. Jewellery by Adrien Mann. Shoes — Jay's own.

BOTH BOYS wear their own clothes.

Guava great time with Bananarama! Our lucky reader Katie Hilliard did and finished up looking peachy — just like one of the fruity bunch who dressed her up and gave her a whole new image!

So blow a raspberry to boring, ordinary looks — and forget about being a gooseberry — fruity beauty is grape fun and you never know . . . Jackie might be able to "orange" it for you! (Ouch! Juice kidding!)

fruity BEAUTIES!

1. This is Katie · · ·

2. this is the band · · ·

. . . and this is what happened!

3. Wish I could see what they're doing!

4. Who mentioned the word loobrush?!

5.

6. & 7. Bananaramazing!

Katie really admires Bananarama's casual, fun-loving style, so she was thrilled when they decided to transform her themselves. Their clothes are basically very simple in colour and idea, but it's the way they're put together and the little individual or eccentric touches that make them special, so Katie really learned a lesson in style!

Bananaramadressing involves lots of loose, comfortable layers — in Katie's case, starting with a plain white sweater. Add a baggy, checked skirt with a fancy belt or a dark pinafore-style frock, belted and bloused at the waist, and you've already got a great basic style!

Then, add the secret ingredients — a wide-brimmed hat, set well back on your head, mittens, cute little ankle boots and home-made legwarmers (cut off a sweatshirt or

Sarah, but this kind of look needn't be expensive or difficult — all you need is a little ingenuity and a good eye for a bargain! Jumble sales, Oxfam or welfare shops are great places to find big sweaters, plain T-shirts or unusual accessories — hats and raiding

you already have, too — the legwarmers - and - sleeveless - top - from - sweatshirt idea is a case in point, and you can certainly add length to a skirt by sewing on an extra panel, maybe in a different colour!

Go for lots of layers, lots of comfort and let your own shine through

Top *Pop* trio

"I ain't what you do, it's the way that you do it..." sang Bananarama and Fun Boy Three in their eponymous 1982 hit.

For superstar 80s trio Bananarama, this was especially true as they featured in "Jackie" on their rise to pop success.

Sara, Siobhan and Keren became as famous for their unique, defiant style as they were for their sharp, catchy records.

Girls, keen for a change from the more traditional teen styles, embraced the lively fashions of this spiky, extrovert trio, bringing fresh trends to high streets everywhere.

"Jackie" magazine was quick to catch on, and featured the girls on the magazine's cover in 1983, where they shared everything from tips on boys to looking great – and how to be the girl you wanted to be!

No. 998 FEBRUARY 19, 1983

THURSDAYS ■ 16p IR 24p (Inc. VAT)

Jackie

FANTASTARAMA!

POP

Modern Romance
A Flock Of Seagulls
Talk Talk

BANANARAMA-STYLE!
A Lucky Reader Learns To Dress With A Difference!

Two Terrific Stories!

BANANARAMA

NOW LOOK HERE!

Have you noticed that hardly anybody wore trousers back then? Sadie looks comfy, feminine and practical in pink top and trousers but Cilla Black's sitting on an elephant wearing a dress! Er . . . perhaps I should rephrase that.

Pink fluffy jumper from Chelsea Girl. Price: £13.99. Assorted sizes and colours. From all branches of Chelsea Girl.

Pink cotton trousers from Freeman's catalogue. Price: £8.99. Sizes: 8-14. Colours: Pink, white, turquoise. From Freeman's catalogue (No. WP8061) or direct from Sue Snowdon, 139 Clapham Road, London.

Flat blue pumps with strap detail from Chelsea Girl. Price: £14.99. Sizes: 3-7. Colours: White, turquoise, black. From selected branches of Chelsea Girl.

Pink scarf from a selection at Debenhams, Oxford Street, London W1 and branches. Prices start from £1.99.

Meet the girls of yesterday and today!
Jackie was always top of the fashion league, even in issue No. 1, and now we've made it to our 1000th birthday, you can see we're still one in a thousand — and the best one, too!

Today's girl — that's you! — wears relaxed, casual clothes, so she can look the way she wants to — she can even create her own trends, instead of toeing the fashion line! There are lots of great individual looks she can try out, so be a modern girl and follow our example.

All the best people have been doing it for years!

Millie (she sang the original version of "My Girl Lollipop — "My Boy Lollipop," of course!) looking smart but casual. (Are you sure you've got the right picture? . . . The Ed.) Well, you should remember . . . Ow!

Rust blouse with V-neck detail from Chelsea Girl. Price: £12.99. Sizes: 10-14. Colours: Assorted. From selected branches of Chelsea Girl.

Full check skirt from Chelsea Girl. Price: £10.99. Sizes: 10-14. Colours: One colour only. From selected branches of Chelsea Girl.

Yellow mesh scarf from a selection at Debenhams, Oxford Street, London W1 and branches. Prices start from £1.99.

Rust suede court shoes from Sacha. Sizes: 3-7. Colours: Rust, black, mustard, grey, burgundy. From Sacha, 351 Oxford Street, London and all branches.

Bare-faced cheek, then and now! (Well, there is a bare face somewhere under the pancake make-up, cake mascara and 6 inches of false eyelashes! When that lot ran, it looked like a relief map of the Highlands!)

Shift dresses were all the rage in 1964 — nowadays they'd be guaranteed to shift anyone about a hundred miles out of your way — especially if you've also got a hairstyle like a demented golly! Styles are sportier and easier to move in nowadays — thank goodness. Wearing this little lot would be like trying to move like Leroy while wearing a starched cardboard box!

Red and grey striped T-shirt from Freeman's catalogue. Price: £3.50. Sizes: 10-16. Colours: One colourway only. From Freeman's catalogue (No. WP9106) or direct from Sue Snowdon, 139 Clapham Road, London.

Grey ra-ra skirt from Freeman's catalogue. Price: £6.99. Sizes: 10-16. Colours: Grey only. Stockists as above.

Grey canvas bootees from Chelsea Girl. Price: £10.99. Sizes: Assorted. Colours: One colour only. From selected branches of Chelsea Girl.

Red canvas bag from Chelsea Girl. Price: £10.99. Colours: Cream, black, red. From selected branches of Chelsea Girl.

7

Sadie . . . has cleansed, ton . . . skin and is all set for . . .

Now set your . . . by applying . . . powder with a . . . off. Choose a . . . loose powder, . . . powder and . . . r face. Then . . . a big soft . . .

Apply . . . hlighter . . . owbone . . . nd blend . . . sponge . . . check . . . match

8

JUDY
JACKIE
CAROLINE
JANIS
SADIE

Get ready to stun 'em this Christmas . . . with tips from the girls who make beauty their business!

SADIE FROST

. . . nise Judy from our . . . ne of our favourite . . . that's bang up to . . . to keep up with the . . . d with her, we found . . . amazingly simple! . . . important in this . . . I always take care . . .

. . . e they arrive at . . . a model turned up . . . hed hair, she'd be . . . again! Judy makes . . . nd soft, giving it a . . . couldn't face . . . d it really . . . girls that the . . . t . . . lot," she . . . the aerobics class . . . a keep-fit fanatic!" . . . work, though, so . . . front of the camera's . . .

. . . ur cover so many times . . . roduce her! She's always . . . so, we wondered, how . . . her hectic lifestyle and . . .

. . . form of exercise," she . . . cs, too. It's essential to . . . ou and up feeling . . . ich her weight . . . Christmas! . . .

Jackie added. "I also floss my teeth — and always take my make-up off before I fall into bed. Apart from waking up with panda eyes, sleeping in make-up's disastrous for your skin!"

Lazy girls, take heed!

CAROLINE

Caroline's one of the most active of the girls we spoke to, and with all the exercise she takes, it's little wonder she can eat what she likes!

"I love dancing," Caroline told us, "and I walk wherever I can, too (much healthier than the smoke-filled bus or tube!) and never diet. I think it's really silly when girls constantly lose and put on weight!"

Caroline wears little make-up, taking great care over her daily skin-care routine.

"I couldn't do without lipstick, either," she explained, "as it can double as a blusher. A brown eye pencil can be used as a lip liner, too — I like versatile make-up items!

Caroline doesn't spend a fortune on beauty products. Christmas is an ideal time to ask for extra-special products that she normally might not buy — but for the rest of the year, Caroline uses the items she has in lots of imaginative ways!

JANIS

Janis is the girl with the amazing mane of hair, and we're sure you'll recognise her from TV ads, as well as our fashion pages in Jackie! Janis told us how she keeps her hair in such super condition.

"Each week I have a conditioning treatment," Janis explained, "when my hair's coated with conditioner and wrapped in silver foil to make . . .

. . . wear sporty styles like tracksuits — in this business they're easy to get in and out of!"

Janis uses bath and shower time as an opportunity to give her body a treat, using lots of baby oil after bathing to keep her skin soft. She rubs coarse salt over her body before a shower, too, as it removes dead skin cells and peps up circulation. After seeing Janis looking super in Jackie, we reckon it's well worth giving her hints a try!

SADIE

Sadie's a great believer in wearing as little make-up as possible to give her skin a chance to "breathe" — as of course, a good skin's essential when you prepare to go foundation-less!

"I like Clinique soap and a light moisturiser, using baby lotion to remove make-up. Foundation can really clog your pores so I never use it!"

Sadie doesn't spend her hard-earned cash on special beauty treatments, and she's only had a facial treatment in a salon once. "That was when I was in the Spandau Ballet video," she explained, "as I had to be completely painted gold. Not the best thing you can do for your skin, I assure you!"

Like Caroline, Sadie makes sure her diet includes all the nutrients she needs. "From time to time, I do diet," she told us, "but for health reasons, not to watch my weight. Eating just fruit, cheese and wholemeal things like rice or bread really does your skin good!"

Sadie striping it rich in a real party style. And a Pearly Queen of the past — Elkie Brooks stars in stripes back in 1964. Can you believe that hair?
Black and white striped silky dress from Freeman's catalogue. Price: £22.95. Sizes: 10-16. Colours: Black and white from Freeman's catalogue direct from

Super Sadie

S HE is known as an actress, producer and fashion designer – a true British creative.

In the 1980s she was already a very familiar face – to "Jackie" girls!

Sadie Frost featured regularly in the "Jackie" fashion and beauty pages in the 80s, and was a much-loved cover girl, her face beaming out beneath that iconic logo on many occasions over the decade.

Sadie became a popular choice for the editors due to her fresh-faced, cheerful looks and, in many ways, was the classic "Jackie" girl.

As a result Sadie was in high demand. In one issue she helped girls create the perfect make-up look for a night out.

In another she modelled the latest trends from the catwalk and high street.

There's no doubt the grounding in glam she got from "Jackie" magazine has stood her in good stead for the showbiz life and career she still enjoys today!

Making-up isn't hard to do. Jan, our Beauty Ed, shows you how...

MAKING FACES

2 If you're lucky enough to have perfect skin you could do without foundation altogether but otherwise it helps even out skin tones and cover up any blemishes. When choosing foundation, test the shade by daylight for the best match. Smooth the foundation over your face and throat with a slightly damp cosmetic sponge using short sweeps.

3 Check your face for any spots or dark circles around your eyes. Stroke concealer on to the areas where you need to use it, either straight from the stick or with a brush. Blend by patting or pressing into your skin — never 'drag' the skin, especially around the eyes. Medicated concealers should help any spots and pimples.

5 Blusher will help give your face a natural glow if applied properly. Using a soft brush, start with the lightest touch then build up until you get the depth of colour you want. If you prefer to use a cream blusher apply it before face powder, blending in well.

6 Before making up eyes, double-check that foundation is smooth, dark rings are camouflaged and all powder has settled. Now attend to your eyebrows. Use an eyeshadow and brush into the eyebrow using a colour just slightly darker than your eyebrow. This evens out the eyebrows and makes them thicker, which is fashionable just now. If brows are sparse fill in with light feathery strokes using an appropriately coloured eyebrow pencil.

7 For basic shaping of eyes use three colours or three shades of one colour. Cream has been used here all over the eye, grey to define the eye along lid and brown to shade the eyelid.

9 Apply mascara with a wand using two thin coats — make sure the first one is dry before applying the second. To prevent clogging, comb through with a little eyelash comb or clean mascara wand — this should get rid of any lumps.

10 Outline your lips with a brush or, if you find it easier use a lip pencil, but keep to the natural outline. Fill in, using a brush, then blot with a tissue to soften the line, then re-apply. You should find that your lip colour will last much longer if you do this.

● The finished look!

Spotted!

THERE are stars and superstars – and then there are megastars! There is no doubt that George Michael and Andrew Ridgeley of Wham! fell into the latter category.

In the early 80s they were the most popular pop act in the world, and the dishy dynamic duo were regulars in the pages of "Jackie".

As popular for their looks as their brilliant tunes, the boys appeared on the cover several times, and were in high demand for their fashion know-how as well as their music.

Featuring in "Jackie" was a step to fame for many celebs over the years. It is impossible to include them all, but flicking through the pages reveals everyone from "Emmerdale" actress Gillian Kearney to actor and presenter Alan Cumming.

"Jackie" holds a special place in the heart of its readers and the many stars who graced its pages.

GILLIAN KEARNEY

NO. 996 FEBRUARY 5, 1983 THURSDAYS 16p IR 24P (Inc. VAT)

Jackie

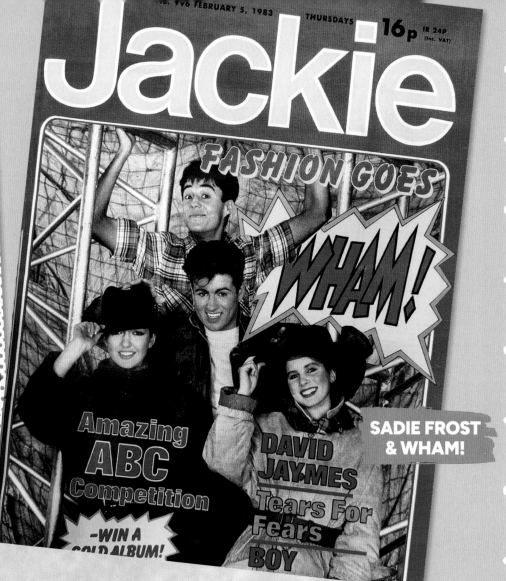

FASHION GOES

WHAM!

Amazing ABC Competition

—WIN A GOLD ALBUM!

DAVID JAYMES

Tears For Fears

BOY

SADIE FROST & WHAM!

4. SUZANNE
Cream vest from Laurence Corner. Price: £5.85. Colours: Assorted.
Mesh scarf — details as before.
Green army trousers from Flip. Price: £11.99. Colours: Khaki, beige.
Brown belt by Pinto Sportswear — details as before.
Red suede boots by Shelly's Shoes — details as before.

eved shirt from £2.50. Colours:
Laurence Corner £1.79 per yard.
and. Adrien Mann. £3.99. Colours: ost major depart- from Laurence

GRANT
N'T BE SEEN
N
THIS

The first look is a soft and floaty. "I love this, it's like some of the stuff my friends make for me. The colours are great, they're so dreamy. Eh, what am I supposed to do with this bow?"

A cropped peach T-shirt has been matched up with blue cotton skirt with braces, and a flared peach skirt is worn underneath. All clothes from a selection at Whyggas.

"I knew as soon as I saw this outfit that I'd like it 'cos I wear a black denim jacket and shirt exactly the same as this in Evoplastic."

Gill's wearing a snow-washed baggy denim jacket and short skirt with a baggy sweat shirt, all from a selection at Chelsea Girl. White ankle socks and black ankle boots (snaffled from the wardrobe department) complete the outfit.

"Oh, yeah, I really like this outfit — it's pretty and summery, just the sort of thing I'd wear myself. The hat's lovely."

And a quick word from Simon O'Brien who oddly enough is passing through the Grants' living room. "She looks great, the hat's all right, innit? Do you think I'd suit it?" Easier, sure Simon!

Gill's adopted a summery sailor look with the blue and white stripey dress and sailor hat from a selection at Top Shop.

Gill's mum (after LOADS of persuasion) joins her daughter in the spotlight.

"Gosh, you can see my stomach in this one! It's really nice, though, I love short skirts like this. In fact I'd like to buy it where did you get it?"

The black and white ribbed top and girly skirt are both from a selection at Top Shop.

Oh, well, that's the end of the fashion 'shoot' and it's time for photographer Sol to pack away all the gear and return the Grants' living room to its true glory. So how did Gill enjoy her day as a Jackie model?

"Mmmmm, well it was really good fun, especially as the clothes were so nice, but I don't think I'd like to do it professionally, or anything. I'd hate to have to stand still for so long and ummmm, I don't actually like getting my picture taken!"

Style Queens

A S the Eighties progressed and we moved into the last decade of the 20th century, "Jackie" lost none of its pulling power, with stars continuing to line up to appear in its pages.

You've "Got To Be Certain" that one of those was Australian pop princess Kylie Minogue, who was as famous for being a style icon as she was for being a purveyor of catchy chart smashes.

Of course, she remains just as popular for both today!

Actress and producer Colette Brown – *EastEnders'* Dr Kennedy – also cut her teeth in the mag during this time.

She grew used to being under the studio lights and in front of the camera on various cover and photo shoots in "Jackie".

CREAM top from a selection at Hennes. Wool skirt; £9.99, from Chelsea Girl. Jumper round shoulders; £14.99, from Top Man

...ng in? Colour yourself in!

DRESS HER

Kylie Minogue is crazy . . . about clothes that is! We invited her along to our favourite photographer's studio so she could tell us for herself.

The first thing that happens when a pop star arrives for a photo session is a consultation with the Jackie styling team. When Kylie arrives two of the "team" are busy discussing the background for the pics . . .

Hmm . . . ahem . . . hmm!
"Hello, I'm Kylie."
"What? Oh, hello, would you like to come and see the clothes we've brought for you to wear?"
"Sure!"

Hurray, Kylie really likes our choice! Sometimes, pop stars hate the clothes sooo much that they refuse to wear them, and sulk all day!
Luckily Kylie isn't like that at all! While Michi (Make-up) and Jane (Hair) decide how they're going to make Kylie look there's time for a quick cup of tea and a chat . . .

Are you sure you don't want something to eat with your tea? (Which, incidentally, fact fans, is white with no sugar!)

"Ha, ha . . . are you going to start telling me I'm too thin? People are *always* saying I'm too thin! Especially the "news"papers! I think I'm the right size and weight for my height!"

Indeed, you are! Do the "news"papers bother you with all of their stories?

"No, not at all! Sometimes I wonder where they get the imagination for them! I don't let it bother me, but if someone wrote something really hurtful I'd be annoyed then."

Who do you admire in British pop music?

"Patsy Kensit looks *really* nice, doesn't she? I love that record she did with the Pet Shop Boys. Rick Astley is really great too, and no, I'm not just saying that because of S/A/W! Patsy's hair looks really brilliant. Which reminds me, I should get mine highlighted again, it's got

really dull since I've been in Britain!"

Well, that's the fabulous British weather for you!

"Yeah, it is really cold just now! I mean I hardly even have a tan at all . . ."

Yes you do! ("Milk-bottle" journalist holds out arm for Kylie to compare.)

"Wow! You really are white! Ah, but it's probably because you're really fair-skinned."

Indeed. So, what else have you been up to — have you been shopping yet?

"I seem to have been so busy, I don't have any time! I've bought a few things but not much. Tell you what, I bought these shoes (a particularly nice pair of red suede "courts") and they're different colours because one was in the window!"

A swizz! You should've taken them back!

"Ha, ha! I haven't had the *time!*"

What do you really hate when you're tired?

"I hate when you've got what seems like 1000 photographers (from the "news"papers, shouting, 'Over 'ere love' and 'Smile, love' at you all at once!"

At this point the photographer, etc., are ready to "go", so Kylie is "whisked" out to face the camera and the Jackie "stylists" make some quick finishing touches . . .

Phew! Finished at last! But there's just one last thing . . . "Er . . . I really like the black leather jacket you brought for me to wear, could I buy it?"

No problem! One phone call later and Kylie escaped from the Jackie team, tired, but happy with a "happening" jacket!

GREY skirt and button-through cardi from a selection by Pamplemousse.

TURQUOISE cord skirt; £9.99, from Chelsea Girl. Cotton shirt; £29.99, from Via Satalite. Woolly hat from a selection at Asda.

CORAL cardi and skirt from a selection at Marks and Spencer. Scarf from a selection at Asda.

BLACK velvet dress; approx. £29.99, from Chelsea Girl.

D. SPENCE

NOV. 21, 1987 Thursday

28p IR 41p (inc. VAT)

Jackie

30p IR 44p (inc. VAT)

Jackie

No. 1290

SEPT. 24, 1988 Thursday

JACKIE GOES DOWN UNDER!
THE BOYS FROM NEIGHBOURS
SCOTT, MIKE & HENRY

KYLIE

WE DRESS HER UP!
PIN UP THE WIZARD OF OZ
MICHAEL HUTCHENCE
PLUS FASHION, BEAUTY, PHOTO STORIES AND TONS MORE!

RAP UP!
FASHION
s of hunk
HOFIELD • MATT DILLON
URAN • DAVID BOWIE

U P

Thanks to:
Sue Foster/Kelly Cooper
Jane (Vidal Sassoon)
Michi (Make-up)
Lesley Goring PR
(Clothes by Johnsons)

MATTERS OF THE Heart

> "I don't know what to do. If only there was someone who could help me. Wait a minute, there is!"

AS well as being the journal of record for young girls, and a fountain of knowledge when it came to all matters fashion and beauty, "Jackie" played a pivotal role in helping its readers navigate that most tricky subject of all – boys!

Whether it was wise advice in the form of the stars, or a quiz to dig deep into the psyche of the male species, "Jackie" was never short of a handy tip.

Certain areas of the magazine are more well remembered than others, and one of the best-loved is the famous photo stories that graced every issue.

These stories do exactly what they say on the tin – they tell a tale, usually of romance and drama, in comic book style panels, which were real people rather than drawings.

Some were standalone stories, some were serialised over several issues to keep readers coming back week after week, but all of them got to the core of an issue that could affect "Jackie" girls.

Warm, witty, but often sharp and serious, too, these stories were created by the "Jackie" staff, who would rope in friends, family and colleagues among others to appear.

Over the years, there were more than a few familiar faces who turned up, too, as you will see over the next few pages. Basically, if you wanted to get that boy of your dreams, "Jackie" was the place to go for advice on how to make it happen!

BETWEEN THE LINES

Jill's pen-friend, Gwynneth, has come to stay with her. But since she arrived, she's been trying to split up Jill and her boyfriend, Mike. And it seems to have worked . . .

THE END

88

Wishing I Was Lucky

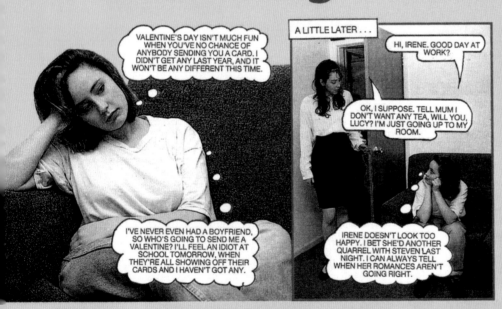

THAT ISN'T EVEN THE WORST OF IT. WHAT ABOUT IRENE AND STEVEN? I — I'VE PROBABLY RUINED EVERYTHING FOR THEM. STEVEN MUST WANT TO MAKE THINGS UP, BUT IRENE WON'T EVEN KNOW. OH, WHY DID I HAVE TO STEAL THAT CARD? IT WAS A CRAZY THING TO DO!

THEN . . .

ARE YOU OK, LUCY?

OH . . . STEWART . . . I — I SUPPOSE YOU'RE WONDERING WHAT'S GOING ON TOO!

I AM, A BIT. I'VE BEEN GETTING A LOT OF FUNNY LOOKS FROM YOUR PALS TODAY. AND I DON'T UNDERSTAND SOME OF THE JOKES THEY'VE BEEN MAKING!

AFTER LUCY EXPLAINED . . .

THERE'S ONLY ONE THING YOU CAN DO, LUCY. YOU'LL NEED TO GIVE THE CARD BACK TO YOUR SISTER. IT SOUNDS LIKE THIS GUY STEVEN'S IMPORTANT TO HER. YOU DON'T WANT TO MAKE THINGS DIFFICULT FOR THEM, DO YOU?

I SUPPOSE YOU'RE RIGHT. SHE'LL BE FURIOUS WHEN I TELL HER, BUT IT'S MY OWN FAULT. I'LL GO STRAIGHT HOME AND SEE HER AFTER SCHOOL.

AND . . .

I'M SORRY, IRENE. I KNOW I SHOULDN'T HAVE DONE IT. I — I WAS JUST FEELING SO MISERABLE 'COS I HADN'T GOT ANY VALENTINES OF MY OWN.

I OUGHT TO STRANGLE YOU, LUCY. I'VE SPENT THE WHOLE DAY THINKING STEVEN HADN'T BOTHERED TO SEND ME A CARD! BUT I'M TOO RELIEVED TO BE ANGRY WITH YOU. I'D BETTER GO TO THE BOWLING ALLEY AND MEET HIM.

WELL, AT LEAST THAT'S SORTED THINGS OUT WITH IRENE. NOW I'D BETTER GO AND FACE THE GIRLS. I'M GOING TO FEEL SUCH A FOOL. THEY'LL NEVER LET ME LIVE IT DOWN.

AND . . .

IT'S NEARLY SIX O'CLOCK. LUCY SHOULD BE HERE BY NOW.

I CAN'T WAIT TO FIND OUT WHO HER BOYFRIEND IS. DO YOU REALLY THINK IT'S STEWART?

NO. I DON'T THINK SHE'S GOT A BOYFRIEND AT ALL. I'LL BET SHE SENT THAT CARD TO HERSELF! WE'LL SOON FIND OUT, ANYWAY.

HELLO, EVERYBODY.

HI, LUCY. WHERE'S THE MYSTERIOUS 'S', THEN?

THAT'S WHAT I WANTED TO TALK TO YOU ABOUT. I — I'VE GOT SOMETHING TO TELL YOU . . .

THEN . . .

SORRY I'M LATE, LUCY. THAT BUS IS NEVER ON TIME, IS IT?

S-STEWART . . .!?

I THINK WE OUGHT TO GO SOMEWHERE DIFFERENT TONIGHT. I'M GETTING A BIT FED UP WITH THIS PLACE, AREN'T YOU?

WHAT? EM . . . YES, I SUPPOSE SO . . .

THANKS, STEWART. THAT WAS REALLY NICE OF YOU. DID YOU SEE THE LOOK ON THEIR FACES? I'D HAVE FELT A COMPLETE IDIOT IF I'D HAD TO ADMIT I DIDN'T GET A VALENTINE AT ALL!

I COULDN'T LET YOU TELL THEM THAT, LUCY. IT WOULDN'T HAVE BEEN TRUE, ANYWAY.

I KNOW IT'S A LITTLE LATE, BUT IT'S STILL VALENTINE'S DAY, ISN'T IT? I WAS GOING TO LEAVE THIS ONE ON YOUR DESK THIS MORNING, BUT I GOT TOO EMBARRASSED AFTER I SAW YOU SHOWING OFF THAT OTHER CARD TO YOUR PALS!

The End

HORSING AROUND!

Speech bubble: SHE LOOKS NICE. I WONDER WHAT SHE'S DOING OUT HERE ALL BY HERSELF? AND LOOKING SO SAD, TOO.

She brightened up when she saw me, though.

Hello! What are you doing wandering about here on your own?

I WAS JUST ABOUT TO ASK YOU THE SAME THING, MY DEAR.

Come on. I'll give you some grass and then we'll see about getting you home.

GRASS AND A CUDDLE FROM A PRETTY GIRL, THIS IS MY LUCKY DAY.

I soon discovered why she was so sad.

Did you know that all boys—yourself excepted, of course—are creeps?

TELL ME MORE, MY DEAR.

So she did . . .

HE BRINGS ME TO A PARTY—THEN STARTS TO CHAT UP SOMEONE ELSE!

I'm not having a very good time, Dave. I'd like to go home.

Suit yourself. There's a bus stop on the corner.

Then there was Scott.

So I'll see you tomorrow, then.

Yes, Scott.

But . .

HE'S NOT GOING TO TURN UP. WHY DID HE SAY HE'D SEE ME AGAIN WHEN HE OBVIOUSLY DIDN'T WANT TO . . .

The next boy she liked a lot. But he went away to college.

I'LL write to you, Alison. I promise.

He didn't, of course. So the fact is, you're the nicest guy I've met in a long time.

AND YOU'RE THE BEST CUDDLER I'VE MET.

Then, of course, what's-his-face had to come along.

Hoi! Stop stuffing that pony with grass! He's fat enough as it is!

CHARMING! YOU CAN ALWAYS COUNT ON ANDY, MY BOSS, TO MESS THINGS UP.

You little pest, Fred! I've told you before about wandering out of the stable on your own!

Pest, is he? Well, if that's how you treat him, no wonder the poor thing tries to escape!

What?

THAT'S RIGHT. YOU TELL HIM, ALISON.

Not that it's any of your business, but let me tell you that Fred here lives like a lord. All he has to do for a living is give little kids rides. I wish I had it as easy!

But she hadn't finished . . .

That's how YOU say you treat him! He probably thinks differently! I may just report you to the RSPCA before I'm finished!

She stalked off in a right state.

Who was that, Fred? And how could you just stand there and let her think I was some kind of monster?

OH, IT WAS EASY, REALLY. MY NATURAL ACTING ABILITY.

She was nice, though. I could quite fancy her. Pity we couldn't have met under different circumstances.

IT WOULDN'T HAVE DONE YOU ANY GOOD, MATE. SHE'S OFF BOYS AT THE MOMENT. SHE LIKES SWEET LITTLE PONIES, THOUGH.

He was a bit quiet over the next few days.

Time to get saddled up, Fred. The kids'll be here soon.

NO CHEERFUL GOOD MORNING. MOST STRANGE.

He seemed to be in a daze half the time.

Andy! Where are you going with Fred? There are no rides this morning!

What? Oh, yes, sorry, Boss. I forgot . . .

Not only that, but he left me outside the wrong stall. I didn't mind that, though . . .

AT LEAST I'M NEXT TO LUCY. THE MOST BEAUTIFUL PONY IN THE WHOLE WORLD. IT MAKES MY MANE CURL EVERY TIME I SEE HER.

hen Dreamy Dan appeared.

HO!! YOU'RE PUTTING MY SADDLE ON THE WRONG WAY ROUND! AND IN FRONT OF LUCY, TOO! SHE MUST THINK I'M A RIGHT TWIT TO HAVE YOU AS A BOSS!

I decided enough was enough. So next time he left me alone . . .

I'VE GOT TO FIND ALISON AGAIN. IF I CAN GET ANDY AND HER TOGETHER, MAYBE THINGS WILL GET BACK TO NORMAL.

I found her in the same place I'd first come across her.

Fred! Have you escaped again?

I DON'T ESCAPE, MY DEAR. I MERELY WALK OUT OF THE YARD AS THE FANCY TAKES ME.

I got a nice cuddle again.

I feel terrible, Fred. A friend of mine told me your boss is a pretty nice guy. I'd like to apologise to him, but there's no way he'd speak to me now.

But wait a minute! I've just thought of a fantastic idea!

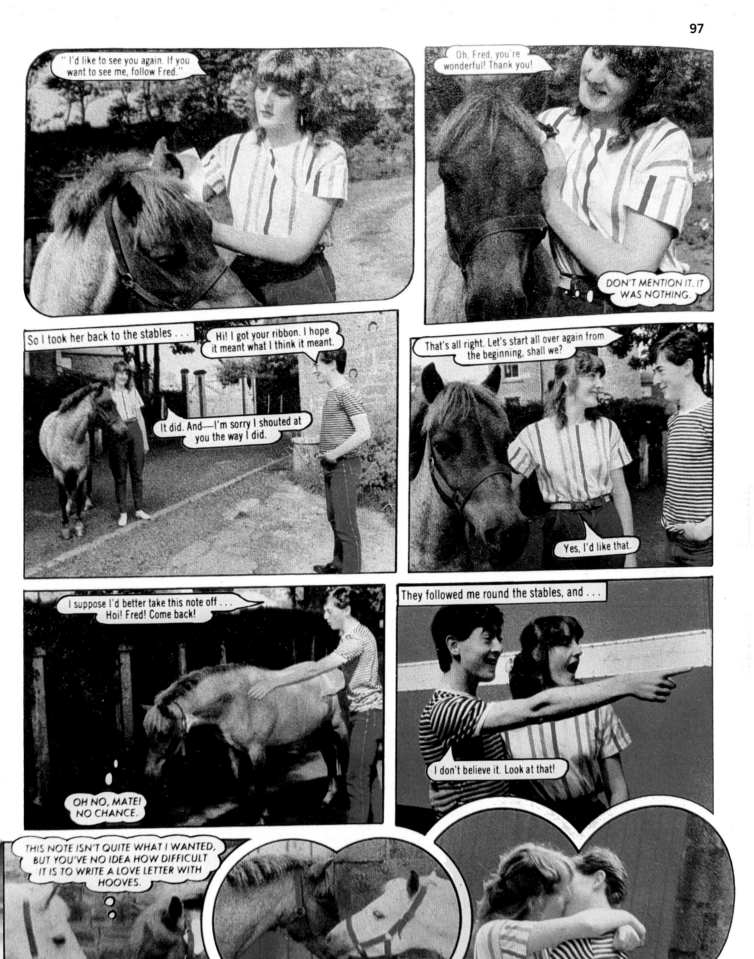

CHOOSE YOUR ANSWERS TO FIND OUT WHAT SORT OF VALENTINE GIRL YOU ARE

A

B

C

How Roma Are

1 WHICH VALENTINE HEART DO YOU LIKE BEST?

(A) Red Victorian-type heart with gold-embossed pattern and bordered around the edges with lovely old lace.

(B) Plain old-gold heart on background of oriental or Indian traditional pattern.

(C) Large exploding heart with beams of light and stars shooting from it in all directions.

(D) Drawing of a biological human heart with the words "thump, thump!" emanating from it.

(E) Picture of a solid gold heart jewelled with diamonds, rubies, emeralds etc.

(F) Heart drawing with modern psychedelic designs.

2 WHAT KIND OF VALENTINE CARD WOULD YOU MOST LIKE TO RECEIVE?

(A) A very romantic flowery one, with the words: "To the one I love with all my heart."

(B) A classical Madonna-like girl's face with the words: "All my love."

(C) A very modern angel with a flirty expression and the words: "You're no angel – but I love you!"

(D) A cute, zany face and the words: "To funny face!"

(E) A picture of a beauty queen in crown and robes and the words: "To the most beautiful girl in the world."

(F) A sun-tanned, laughing girl's face and the words: "To my sunshine girl."

5 WHICH ANONYMOUS VALENTINE CARD WOULD YOU MOST LIKE TO BE SENT FROM SOMEONE WHO ADMIRES AND LOVES YOU FROM AFAR?

(A) A card crammed with hearts and flowers in lovely pastel shades.

(B) A classical-type painting of a Greek goddess.

(C) A drawing of six boys with bouquets, all down on their knees in front of one beautiful girl.

(D) A funny cartoon-style cupid shooting arrows.

(E) A picture of a huge bouquet of orchids.

(F) A picture of a brick wall with graffiti-type hearts and arrows chalked on it.

6 WHICH CARD WOULD YOU CHOOSE FOR YOUR VALENTINE, IF YOU WANTED TO SUIT IT TO HIS CHARACTER?

(A) A knight in shining armour, sword in hand.

(B) The famous statue of "The Thinker".

(C) A loveable-looking boy with a wicked expression but a halo around his head.

(D) A clown.

(E) A dramatic picture of a mysterious cloaked figure in a mask.

(F) A friendly-looking boy on a motorbike?

ntic You?

Well? Is February 14 the most important day of your life? Or do you think it's just the day after February 13 and you can't see what all the fuss is about? Either way, try our quiz and find out how romantic you **REALLY** are. You could be surprised!

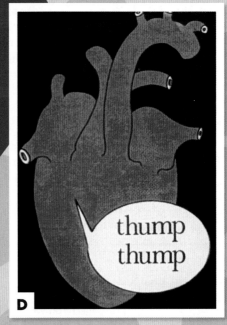

D

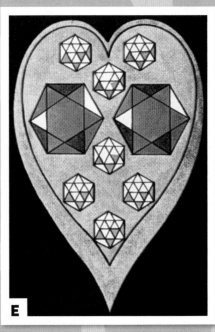

E

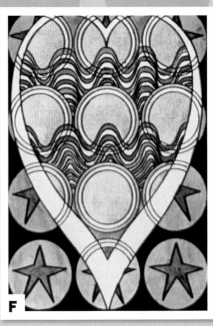

F

3 THESE ARE THE PRINTED MESSAGES INSIDE SIX VALENTINE CARDS. WHICH ONE WOULD YOU CHOOSE TO SEND TO YOUR BOYFRIEND?

(A) "To my love, my life, my whole world."
(B) "My heart and soul are yours."
(C) "To my best boyfriend. . . the other 364 don't mean a thing to me – honest!"
(D) "I'm sending you a Valentine as you're such an ugly old mug, no-one else will!"
(E) "My love for you is as deep as the seas and as strong as the mighty mountains."
(F) "To the best boy in the whole world – from the girl who loves you."

7 WHICH VALENTINE'S CARD DO YOU THINK WOULD SUIT YOUR CHARACTER BEST?

(A) A beautiful Cinderella-like princess with golden ringlets.
(B) A ballet dancer in a graceful pose.
(C) A wild, barefooted gypsy girl.
(D) A mad, zany girl floating up into the sky, holding onto a bunch of balloons.
(E) A girl in a long 30s-style dress, reclining on a sofa.
(F) A healthy-looking outdoor girl.

4 WHICH VALENTINE SERENADE WOULD YOU PREFER?

(A) Romeo singing with all his heart underneath your balcony.
(B) A solitary violinist, looking terribly soulful and absorbed.
(C) A Spanish guitarist.
(D) David Essex.
(E) A sexy singer in a really smooth suit.
(F) A cowboy sitting on a fence with his guitar.

8 WHICH VALENTINE COUPLE APPEALS TO YOU MOST?

(A) A couple in evening dress by a moonlit fountain.
(B) A couple holding hands beside an ancient temple.
(C) A couple dancing at a lively party.
(D) A madly happy couple jumping for joy on a trampoline.
(E) A couple on stage, enacting a dramatic love scene.
(F) A couple running hand in hand along the surf on a deserted beach.

Now count which letter you scored most and read the conclusions overleaf . . .

MOSTLY (A)

You're a really romantic Valentine girl – feminine, dreamy, loving and lovable. You need a boy you can really respect and look up to, and that shouldn't be difficult, because you'd make any boy feel ten feet tall. You have lots of feminine charms, sympathy and understanding. Your love life and emotions are very important things to you, and your heart definitely rules your head. For you, romance makes the world go round – but a little caution might be a good thing sometimes because it does prevent a broken heart!

MOSTLY (B)

You don't love lightly. Your feelings go very deep and your emotions are unfathomable. Probably not many boys will spark your interest because you have very high standards, but once you find your true love, it will be a very deep, real relationship. When you fall in love, you really fall! Superficial relationships are a waste of time for you. You have a great deal of love to give and an abundance of emotional honesty. Your head usually rules your heart, but don't be surprised if you're swept off your feet one day!

MOSTLY (C)

Let's face it, you're a flirt! You want variety, entertainment, excitement and a super bloke for every occasion. You live life to the full, but your feelings are sometimes superficial and you're not ready for a really deep relationship yet. With your energy and your flirty ways, your life must be an enviable social whirl. A bit more cool might be a good thing in your dealings with boys though. One day you might just get caught at your own game. But meantime, you live for the moment, so carry on having fun and being a flirt until life and love become more serious!

MOSTLY (D)

All that romantic slop about love isn't for you! Life is fun, and love is wonderful, but you don't believe in going all moody over it. You'd rather have a laugh than an intense emotional encounter and your ability to turn everything into a glorious great joke must make you popular with all those boys who have suffered the rigours of emotional girlfriends. You're great company, a real sport and the kind of girl any boy would be delighted to take out. You're a really happy-go-lucky, glad-to-be-alive Valentine girl! Stay that way!

MOSTLY (E)

You're the Valentine girl to surpass all others. You crave glamour, sophistication and a lifestyle to go with it. You'd like to be a great star with flocks of men gasping at the very sight of you. You frankly expect rather a lot! But then, glamour is in rather short supply these days, and you might just get away with it. You over-dramatise yourself and your feelings, and although you're great at putting on an act, and simply oozing sex appeal, you must admit you're not always genuine. You exaggerate most things, and you must always be the centre of attention. If the act works, you're very fortunate and life must be a fabulous experience, but if you find boys see through the bluff, tone it down a bit. You've got what it takes so there's no need to overdo it!

MOSTLY (F)

You're every boy's idea of a Valentine girl. You have the genuine qualities boys look for and find attractive in a girl. You're fun and lively without being embarrassing, and loving without being sentimental. You're sensible in your approach to love, with the emotional honesty and sincerity to enter into really loving relationships. Boys know where they are with you, because you don't put on any acts. They also respect you because you're feminine enough to be a super Valentine, but also cool and hard-headed enough to stick up for yourself and avoid getting carried away by any old chat. You're not as romantic as some, but in the end you have what counts – you're yourself, a real girl among all the glitter and pretence.

LOVE LETTERS

This thoughtful short story ran in issue 1291, from October, 1988.

A TEARFUL SHORT STORY BY BARBARA JACOBS THAT READS BETWEEN THE LINES.

KERRY flicked through the letters half-blinded by tears, picking out phrases and sentences. "My dearest love, only two hours since you left, I can't wait the eight hours before I see you again." "I know that I could never live without you."

The blue ribbon which held the letters together lay discarded on the bedroom floor. She held the flimsy sheets of paper in her hand, paper that lied and cheated, made promises that were never kept.

Whatever happened to a love that would never die? Whatever happened to "the first moment I saw you I knew I'd never let you go"?

She remembered that first meeting, the beautiful clear day, the scent of roses and wallflowers in the park. She lay feeling the sun warm on her face, making wishes about the approaching summer. And one of the wishes had come true.

A shadow fell between her eyes and the sun, and a gruff voice had started to shout.

"Is this your dog, because he's . . ."

When she sat up, Simon was standing there, his anger turning to stammering as she blinked in the sunshine and ran her fingers sleepily through her tangled curls.

First of all she noticed Buster, her dog, dropping a tennis ball proudly at her side, and then the boy, in tennis shorts and T-shirt, tall, tanned and blushing, reaching out his hand for it.

"He's been ruining your game?" she remembered asking apologetically.

"Well . . . it's OK . . . really . . ." the boy had muttered.

Something strange seemed to be happening. There he was, a racket dangling from his hand, but making no move to reach for the ball which now rolled towards his feet.

And there she was, sleepy-eyed, awakening from dreams, unable to move, as if she feared that any movement might disturb this dream come true. Both stared.

His eyes were bright blue, despite his dark hair. They were blue like summer skies, almost smiling, almost afraid to. There was a stillness around them like the stillness of a stopped clock.

"I'm Simon," he said.

"I'm Kerry."

At first she could hardly believe it, that meeting, the way he'd sat and talked until his tennis partner, a disgruntled boy with red hair and freckles, had come to find him. But before he left, he'd asked for her phone number, and had phoned the moment she walked through the door.

Her mother had smiled and said, "It's someone called Simon. He's phoned twice in the last quarter of an hour," as she handed the phone to her.

It was beautiful. It was amazing. It was exactly as those letters said, the most surprising and overwhelming emotion that had ever hit either of them. From the moment in May when she'd looked up into the sunlight to see those clear blue eyes looking down at her, her life had changed for ever.

Now she wasn't just fairly ordinary Kerry picking out pictures from magazines to pin up and fall in love with, not the Kerry who had wandered into town to browse at the record shop on Saturday morning hoping that the trendily distant boy who worked there would notice her some day. Now she was half of a couple, and the boy who

walked at her side, cradling her hand in his, was worth a million faded rock stars and spotty record store assistants.

Simon shared her jokes, listened to her worries, reassured her through exam nerves, made her feel wanted and needed and extraordinary. And he'd felt like that, too, hadn't he?

She read another fragment of another letter, wiping her eyes dry so as to concentrate on every tender word . . .

"I won't ever change. I know that some boys like to take love and throw it away, hoping that the next time it'll be better. But I believe that love is something that grows and becomes more precious the longer you hold on to it.

"I'm going to hold you, and hold you, and moment by moment, week by week, you grow more precious to me, and always will."

The tears welled again. How could those words have come to nothing? But they had.

She'd noticed Simon losing interest. For weeks it hadn't been anything she could quite put her finger on, just little things. He didn't always look at her when he spoke to her, but straight ahead, as if looking into a future that didn't include her.

He phoned less often. In the early days, he'd call as soon as he arrived home, after seeing her home, to wish her sweet dreams.

Her mum said he had other things on his mind, with the exam results coming out and thinking about college courses, or staying on at school, or trying to get a job.

That was right enough, because he talked of nothing else, and to be honest, it got on her nerves after a while.

She'd say, "See what your results are like before you start worrying,"

and he'd snap, "How would you understand? You haven't had this to face yet. There's more to life than parties and pictures!"

And although she wanted to say, "Yes, I know, I want to help," she knew he didn't really want her help. He wanted to be with the others from his year at school, all the other nailbiters waiting for the results of the exams.

He wanted to be with Gail. She'd find the two of them bunched up in a corner at parties, running through the thousand and one possibilities that the next few days' post might bring.

And today, finally, he'd said, "Listen, Kerry, this isn't working out. Don't think I didn't love you. I did. But everything changes. There are other things I have to do.

"I'm sorry – I'll let you know what happens with my results, if you like. But I've got to keep my options open, now. You do understand, don't you?"

She'd tried. She really had. But there was an image of Gail, standing between her and the sunshine, there were the broken promises, there were the tender words that meant nothing. And there were the letters in her hand.

Hearing her mother's key in the lock, she pushed the letters hurriedly back into their blue ribbon and shoved them into the suitcase under the dead memories of long ago: a brightly patterned kaftan, a pair of scuffed platform shoes, some flared paisley trousers, a yellow mini-dress – all her mum's belongings from before she'd met and married Dad. Old love letters from an old flame that had flickered and died. They belonged in history, with platform soles and flares.

She closed the case, pushed it back under her mum's bed, and crept out of the bedroom just as her mum called up the stairs.

"Kerry! I'm home."

She raced down, and flung herself into her mum's arms. Her mum would understand. First love dies hard.

"You do understand, don't you, Margaret?" that last letter had said. "Someday, believe me, you'll find someone else."

What first attracts you to a boy? Is it his smile, his looks, his money (!) or maybe it's the way he dresses? If it's a boy's clothes that first catch your eye, then you'll no doubt have discovered that the smartest clothes don't necessarily go with the smartest guy! If you want to tell what he's really like by the clothes he wears – then we've got all the answers here! Read on to find out if he's a smoothie or a sweetie – and, what's more important, find out what kind of girl he's likely to go for! And next time you're at the disco and fancy some guy in tight leather jeans and a white T-shirt – well, just remember what we've told you!

THE SMOOTHIE

What he'll wear

The smoothie thinks he's a knockout. He plans his clothes down to the last stitch in his turn-ups and he keeps everything cleaned and well pressed (or rather he supervises his mum, who does it for him). He stopped wearing flared trousers about two years ago, has gone through the plastic beach sandal number, and is now into carefully-toning pastels — especially pinks and greys. He doesn't like to go out in a strong wind or downpour because that would mess up his neat, lightly lacquered hair-do.

What he's like

The smoothie is, above all, fussy. He's spent a lot of time and care on his appearance, and as far as he's concerned, *you* ought to have done the same. He doesn't like heavy kissing and cuddling sessions in case you crease his shirt or leave lipstick on his jacket and he'd be worried to see you drinking ginger beer and blackcurrant rather than nice, non-staining water. He tends to be on the mean side because buying silk shirts is a bit of a financial drain. His conversation is pretty dull and punctuated with cries of, "Watch what you're doing with that lipstick!" or, "Keep that cat away!" He's a pretty good disco dancer, though — mainly because he spends hours practising in front of the mirror.

His kind of girl

The smoothie wants a smart, pretty girl who's not going to outdo *him*. He'll hate her if she's better at disco dancing than he is but she'll need to be quite good so she doesn't embarrass him. He likes going to the movies to note what the stars are wearing these days, and to learn some good lines to come up with. (His girlfriend is expected to fall over in admiration when he does so.) The smoothie hates overweight, sloppy girls, bare feet, sudden displays of affection, and spontaneous pie-throwing contests!

THE STUDENT

What he'll wear

How the student looks is usually totally predictable, as he has only one pair of jeans and a T-shirt for summer and a sweater for winter. It would be of no surprise to anybody, including himself, if he appeared one day in his pyjamas (if he owns any, which is doubtful) because getting dressed is the very least of his worries. His clothes are usually dirty. When he does get around to washing them he'll wrap himself in a blanket in the launderette while he does so. His pockets are usually bulging with paperbacks, notebooks and old sweetpapers. He does not possess a comb. He wears the same Army surplus overcoat come rain or shine.

What he's like

He's enthusiastic and fun to be with, provided you can listen avidly or are prepared to discuss whatever it is he's studying. He loves parties and dancing (which he does enthusiastically but badly) and doing fun, spontaneous things like climbing lamp-posts at 3 a.m. He's generous but broke.

His kind of girl

He's not too fussy. He likes a bit of brain, but usually doesn't notice how you look — which can be pretty infuriating if you've just spent hours and pounds on it. If you like boogieing at expensive discos and eating at expensive restaurants, he's not the man for you. On the other hand, if you like cold baked beans . . . He's neither demanding, attentive nor jealous. If you're the same, then you'll love him. If you're not — steer clear!

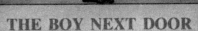

THE BOY NEXT DOOR

What he'll wear

You see him at least half a dozen times every day of your life and you probably wouldn't even fancy him if you were the last two survivors on a desert island. So it's not surprising that you don't rate his appearance much. The boy next door is obliging, in that he mainly wears what his mum puts out for him, which is a pretty unadventurous mixture of V-neck sweaters, cardigans with buttons and rather nasty lace-up shoes. He has his hair cut too regularly, so that his ears are always on show, will have a big bottom before he's much older, and smiles annoyingly and a lot.

What he's like

He's infuriatingly *nice.* Your mum thinks he's "such a nice boy" and he's always to be seen doing toady things like errands, walking his aunt's poodle, cleaning the car and taking neighbours' children to the swings. He's asked you out since time immemorial and you've gone when you're absolutely desperate. Deep down you're quite fond of him, but he does *annoy* you so much. He does dreadful things like whistling, winking and opening the gate for you when he *knows* you've gone through the hole in the hedge since you were six.

His kind of girl

You suspect he might want it to be you, but that's too awful to contemplate. He's so forgiving, *so* generous, *so* undemanding and *so* kind that he'd probably gallantly escort the fat lady from the circus out for an evening if she asked him to! He's almost impossible to put down, so he would basically go out with anybody or anything — which isn't very flattering for *you.*

NG?

THE BIKER

What he'll wear

Something oily. The bike freak is in love with his machine, and for ninety per cent. of his spare time he looks awful. He'll be in dirty overalls with spanners sticking out of them at all angles, he'll have a radio jammed halfway between two stations on the ground nearby, and he'll be whistling tunelessly through his teeth and uttering groans as he administers to his beloved bike. When dressed up (usually to go somewhere on his machine) he'll dress the part in leathers and boots and he can really look quite tasty — if you can ignore the oil in his eyebrows and fingernails, that is!

What he's like

His mind is full of mechanical ideas and dreams of fantastic bikes and he spends most of his time trying to perfect the workings of his own machine. He loves the cheerful sound of spanners clanking in his pockets, and though he likes the company of girls, he'll usually work it so that he takes you to a movie with some car chases in it, or (worse still) to a race meeting.

His kind of girl

If you were decked out from top to toe in bike leathers and reclining in an inviting position on the pillion he *might* notice you, but the biker can't really relate to ladies who don't share his enthusiasms, and you'd have to be pretty smitten by him to put up with them otherwise. He's a definite no if you think a Norton Commando is some sort of Action Man doll and if you hate travelling in anything more uncomfortable than a Rolls-Royce . . .

THE BORE

What he'll wear

You can rumble a bore at a hundred yards by the way he looks. He's usually tall and gangly and he stoops. His hair is usually dirty with — alas — dandruff and he wears clothes that are so out of date, they're almost back in. Things like pale brown Crimplene trousers that are baggy at the bum and so short that a large expanse of ankle,in mustard or leaf green socks, shows. He always wears socks under sandals in the hottest summer, and V-neck jerseys under jackets in winter.

What he's like

He rarely smiles. If he, on a rare occasion, laughs at one of his own jokes, it's such a peculiar high-pitched noise that everybody starts looking to see who's stepped on the cat. He usually talks rather loudly so that people can hear what he says, but they soon stop listening because it's so boring. He's unbelievably mean, and can make a half pint of lager last four hours. He talks about mind-bogglingly boring things like gardening, his relatives, his investments, his spots . . .

His kind of girl

The extraordinary thing about the bore is that he's usually the randiest thing on two legs. He pursues girls like there's no tomorrow, and is usually highly selective and pursues the really glamorous ones who wouldn't look at him twice . . . no, once! Because he's so thick skinned, it's difficult to make him register the word *no*, or even less polite combinations of two words. He's not at all attracted to dull ladies, which is a shame, because they could have some really memorable conversations . . .

THE FITNESS FREAK

What he'll wear

He's usually out of breath but pretending not to be, because he runs to meet you and spends the few minutes it takes you to open the front door, jogging on the step. He's breaking in his new training shoes. The fitness freak cannot *bear* to waste a moment. He does exercises at bus stops, under desks, in the cinema. He's rather red faced, has a large bottom, huge shoulders, and loads of muscles. He's quite indifferent to his clothes, but looks good in jeans and shirts and cowboy boots, or trainers.

What he's like

He's good company because he's energetic and loves to get out and about. This might mean hearty walks or climbs, but he will settle for the cinema if it's a scary film where he can put a strong arm round your shoulders. He loves discos because he sees them as a workout where he can lose all sorts of calories. He might make you jog there, though. He eats an enormous amount, and drinks a lot of beer, which is why he *needs* to jog everywhere! He tells lots of jokes, mostly dirty, and laughs a lot.

His kind of girl

She must be a girl who would be prepared to stand on the touchline for any number of sports most Saturday afternoons. She would have to be able to work a stopwatch, tell him critically about his footwork, and *not* sit huddled in the car with a Thermos of coffee. Funnily enough, he isn't attracted to glamorous girls, because he thinks they're self-obsessed, and because *he* is, he knows about it! He likes slightly sporty, slightly boyish girls who look good in jeans and sweaters, can run fast — and who give as good as they get!

JACKIE SPECIAL . . .

First off, it's not such a great idea to kiss a boy you're not all that interested in, even if he is great to look at. If you don't *like* him then you won't like kissing him, it's as simple as that. For any kiss to work, there's got to be some feeling behind it, so try not to kiss just any boy, especially pushy ones who try to Half-Nelson you into doing it, or you'll only end up regretting it and feeling really let down. Remember — your kisses are precious, they ought to be full of honest feeling, definitely not to be wasted on SLOBS!

OK? Now on to the fascinating subject of kissing and how to kiss . . .

YOU'VE probably imagined what it's like to kiss a boy. In your dreams, everything will be just perfect . . . In real life, though, it might not work out like that, so don't be too let down if it isn't all sweetness and light straight off. Here are a few tips to make all your first kisses that little bit special. Of course, there's no one right way to kiss but the following points to remember might help you out when it comes to the crunch, when he wants to kiss you and you think you might panic and run away from him!

HOW TO KISS

★ *Be prepared for the fact that he probably* **will** *try to kiss you after he's walked you home, although it could happen any time, any place – at the bus stop, in the disco, in the street . . . It'll help if you remember he's just as nervous as you are, so . . .*
★ *Take a few deep breaths and try to relax.*
★ *Keep your head up, don't stare at the ground.*
★ *Look at him.*
★ *When he moves towards you, don't back away.*
★ *Tilt your head.*
★ *Contact! Your lips meet.*
★ *Move your lips with his, slowly.*
★ *Depending on how things are going, you can stop kissing him now and lay your head on his shoulder. That's all there is to it!*

Your Jackie Guide To... Kissing!

Kiss your mum and tell her how much you appreciate her. Kiss your dad and tell him you think he's great. Kiss your boyfriend and *you don't have to tell him a thing* because here, actions speak much louder than words!

There are kisses and kisses though, and no two kisses are alike – a friendly peck on the cheek, for instance, is a million miles from a wild passionate mouth-to-mouth clinch! So which kind of kiss should you use where and with whom, and, when you get right down to it — how should you kiss a boy in the first place anyway? Read our extra-special blue print on all you need to know about kissing and you'll find out!

Once you're with a real, live boy, you ought to find everything goes really smoothly. Just make sure you *like* the boy you're kissing in the first place.

IF YOU DON'T LIKE HIM

If you've only been out with a boy once, and he's taken you home, obviously expecting a late-night snogging session, things can be a bit awkward, especially if you don't want to encourage him. So, once you get to your front door, thank him for a really nice evening, say you'll see him around, then peck him lightly on the cheek, if you like, and go indoors.

Don't allow him to put his arms around you in the first place if you don't want him to, and don't let him kiss you at all if you don't want him to — it'll only make him think you really do like him. So be honest with boys, especially the boys who are nice, not pushy, but whom you don't really fancy.

IF YOU DO LIKE HIM, AND HE LIKES YOU

Here, you'll probably expect your first kiss with him to be out of this world. If it isn't, put it down to nerves and try again. The chances are, though, that your first kiss with a boy you like *will* be wonderful, simply because it's *him* you're kissing!

IF HE WON'T TAKE NO FOR AN ANSWER

If he's too pushy, and he tries to force you to kiss him and you don't really want to, you'll have to tell him to stop. A lot of boys just don't know what's expected of them and so they go completely over the top, especially on first dates. How do you handle a boy like this? You do *not* just stand there and let him do whatever he pleases, that's for sure! You teach him to kiss naturally, the way *you* want to be kissed.

Try to make a joke out of it — say something like, "That may be OK for a female gorilla but I'm a girl." Or simply tell him what he's doing isn't welcome. Ask him to cool it. Or be honest, and tell him you don't *like* it, and will he please stop.

There's absolutely no point whatsoever in pretending to like being kissed in a certain way if you really don't, so for goodness' sake say so. Your boyfriend will probably be glad of it because then he'll stop having to live up to a big he-man image.

KISSING AND LOVEBITES

A lot of girls think lovebites are great and a lot of girls think they're pretty ugly. A lot of boys think that once they give a girl a lovebite that she's his property, while a lot of boys are really turned off by girls with lovebites.

Well, it's up to you really. Most people think kissing is a pretty private and special thing, not something you tell the whole world about. Really, though,

lovebites aren't pretty at all. And do you *really* want your boyfriend to act as if he owned you?

Too obvious lovebites can cause a lot of upsets anyway — your friends think you're a show-off, other boys think of you as being not quite nice, maybe even a bit easy, and as for your parents — it'll hurt them a lot. So is it worth it?

If you don't want lovebites, then tell your boyfriend so.

FRENCH KISSING

French kissing is when you put your tongue into your boyfriend's mouth and he puts his into yours. To a lot of people it's nice and natural. To others it's disgusting. Some people aren't disgusted by it but still don't quite like it.

If *you* don't like it, don't do it, and don't let your boyfriend force you into doing it. He may just be doing it because he thinks that's what you expect or because he thinks it's more grown up, or even a tiny bit daring.

It can be embarrassing to talk openly about your feelings when it comes to the physical side of your relationship with a boy but it's always best to air your views rather than to carry on feeling used and miserable in silence.

So speak up. If there was something he didn't like about you, wouldn't you rather he told you? At least that way, you'd understand each other a whole lot better, and feel even closer than ever.

WHICH KISS SHOULD YOU USE WHERE . . . AND WITH WHOM?

THE FRIENDLY PECK ON THE CHEEK

Use it on a boy you don't want to get serious with. If your evening out together proved a disaster, or even just OK, it's ideal — friendly without being *too* friendly.

THE ROMANTIC KISS

Use it when you're with a boy you really like — one you think you might even get to love!

THE FRENCH KISS

Kiss a boy this way and it ought to mean you've known the boy for some time. French kissing on a first date is a bit pointless and not much fun at all. A lot of boys think you must be pretty experienced if you kiss like this. Well, are you? And can you handle the kind of boy it'll encourage . . . ?

Finally, here are a few do's and dont's to remember. Follow them and you'll keep your kisses really sweet!

Don't *chatter on and on and on because you're nervous at the thought of him kissing you – he'll only think you don't want him to kiss you.*

Do *close your eyes when he kisses you. You don't want any distractions!*

Don't *get into a really heavy session with someone you don't really care about.*

Do *smile or laugh it off if everything does go drastically wrong, if you gulp really loudly, or if your false tooth falls out! Show him you've got a great sense of humour and he'll come back for more . . . and more!*

With Christmas over and the New Year upon us most people are beginning to wonder what 1981 has in store for *them*. We've had a look at what's in the stars for the coming year so that you can see what's likely to come your way!

Read our special Astro forecast for 1981 and see if it's going to be a special year for you!

A Jackie Astro Special

WHAT'S IN STORE FOR YOU IN 1981?

ARIES
(March 21-April 20)

A new moon on March 6 rings the changes and there are a lot of new beginnings in 1981. This will be a year of ups and downs with the emphasis on new relationships and new partnerships.

Your love life is likely to be very hectic with you making all the moves. Don't rush ahead with over-ambitions plans until the second half of the year, otherwise disaster could result!

You'll be on top form as far as health is concerned and there could be a surprise money lift around September. The best and most fortunate month of the year will be April and, if you are thinking of holidays, June will be your best time for travel.

Take care to avoid minor accidents and confrontations with authority in November.

Lucky birthday is April 5.

TAURUS
(April 21-May 20)

As an earth sign you will have a year when tact and diplomacy will play a big part in your life. In 1981 you may find yourself acting as a go-between for your friends, but there is more than a hint of happiness in your own personal affairs.

May is a good month for romance with Venus influencing your stars and September and October are almost as good. Avoid family quarrels at any time, as you may come off second best.

Late summer is an excellent time for saving and putting your plans into action.

Lucky birthday — May 6.

GEMINI
(May 21-June 20)

The early part of 1981 will have lots of restrictions from parents and others in authority for many air sign Geminis, because of the influence of Jupiter. This will cause a few upsets at home and means that you'll have to watch your spending.

Romance is extremely well starred

this year with lots of new faces and friendships. A long-term relationship may fade out but it won't really be all that important in your life.

The social scene is good around April and May and entertaining could bring you to change your mind about a certain boy. Correspondence and invitations bring favourable news, and July is especially lucky for holidays and for finding bargains.

Lucky birthday is June 4.

CANCER
(June 21-July 21)

Your stars show an upward trend to 1981 for everything to do with your love life, but watch out for petty jealousies and gossip in March. Avoid arguments at home during May and be as co-operative as you can to keep the peace.

Travel in June and July will be very

successful. Your social life should receive a boost in May and if you have any secret ambitions or dreams these may be realised in September.

Hobbies and sports are well starred in the winter months, but don't over-tire yourself towards the end of December — reserve your energy for the festive season.

Lucky birthday is July 6.

LEO
(July 22-Aug. 21)

1981 is a good year for friendships for all Leos and there could be a special one in January. Avoid money problems and *don't* borrow, or you could find yourself in hot water.

Your social life is on the up and up

with the best month of the year for your popularity being August. Home affairs are favourably starred especially during the winter months, and romantic friendships are hectic and exciting around the end of July.

Possibly not a year for making ambitious plans but your personal life is satisfactory with lots of happiness and fun. July 25 and August 1 are the two luckiest birthdays, and any trips or holidays should be undertaken during those months.

VIRGO
(Aug. 22-Sept. 21)

No major changes for you this year except that a secret dream or hope may be realised during August. Take care that you don't rock the boat at home during May and avoid any friction with your best friend then.

Restraint with your money will pay off as this is not the best year for spending sprees. There's a distinct possibility that you may have to take on some extra responsibility and this could be tied up with young people or relatives.

Social and outdoor activities are favourably influenced in September and October. Luckiest birthdays are August 26 and 28.

Your love life produces some explosive situations and is full of exciting new happenings.

LIBRA
(Sept. 22-Oct. 22)

You should find yourself being looked after extremely well by your family and friends this year. Romantic trends are happy and uncomplicated with the emphasis on one special person in your life in early spring.

Holidays are best taken in late summer, early autumn, and September is very well starred. Letters, phone calls, and correspondence will bring you many invitations this year and your popularity should be high.

Watch out for minor accidents through carelessness in May and keep an open mind about making changes then. Lucky birthdate is September 1 and your lucky colour is yellow.

SCORPIO
(Oct. 23-Nov. 21)

Your year is divided into three phases in 1981. Early spring is favourable for romance and special friendships, summer is ideal for travel or holidays, and finding out more about yourself, winter brings you success in everything you do.

Avoid upsetting someone close to you in September as it could cause a serious split. Tuesday will be a good day during the year to make decisions and go places.

Adventurous propositions will be coming your way during the autumn months. Luckiest birthday is November 5 and your lucky colour is red.

SAGITTARIUS
(Nov. 22-Dec. 21)

Jupiter, your ruling planet, plays a little havoc with you this year and signs of some difficulties in 1981 are starred, although as the year develops, your stars improve. Romance and special friendships go well in January

and March with the emphasis on long-term friendships.

You are moving into a period of change and may have to take on a few responsibilities at home, school or work. Travel and trips are starred for June and July, and sports, games or physical activities take up a fair amount of time.

A proposal comes as a surprise in the autumn and there could be a friendship that's short lived.

Lucky birthday — December 15.

CAPRICORN
(Dec. 22-Jan. 19)

Saturn, your ruling planet, is in the sign of Libra through 1981 and this should bring you reasonably good all-round luck. Your love life receives lots of boosts and there is a strong romantic link indicated in the early spring.

Relatives and those close to you claim

a lot of your time during May. Extra care may be needed to deal with a friend in July who needs your help.

Wear your lucky birthstone, the garnet, to attract good fortune and your lucky day of the week is Saturday.

Lucky birthday is January 4.

AQUARIUS
(Jan. 20-Feb. 18)

Some disrupting elements in your stars mean that this year minor arguments and other conflicts could disturb the peace. On the whole though, the year should be a social and romantic success.

The moon's influence means that all travel, and holidays in particular, are extremely well starred during July and August. At school or work there could be some promotion, and a boost to your finances around November is likely.

Any new romantic developments in the winter are destined to bring new friendships and happiness! Luckiest birthdays are January 22 and February 7.

PISCES
(Feb. 19-March 20)

The position of Jupiter in your stars this year brings excellent chances for those who want to make their mark on the world. If you have any ideas for new schemes you want to get off the ground, now is the time to do so!

June and July is a lucky time for family affairs with everyone getting on with everyone else. May is an excellent time for short trips or holidays but March is a month for minor upsets.

Your birthstone is the bloodstone and your lucky number this year is 4. February and March is the time when your confidence will be increased as some of those daydreams could come true.

Lucky birthdays are February 27 and March 13.

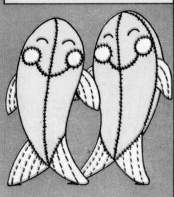

So there you are — your special guide to what's in store for you in 1981! But we hope that, whatever your stars say, 1981 is going to be the best year ever for you!

Word TO THE WISE

Dear Cathy & Claire

Dear Ellie

talk it over

THE pages of "Jackie" are invariably remembered with great affection, but there was one feature that is recalled more fondly than most. The Cathy & Claire page was the hot favourite in the magazine and the one to which most readers turned first. It was something to be devoured over with friends, such was the relatability of the problems dealt with therein.

The subjects covered were always relevant to the readers – the boys they had crushes on, the trials and tribulations of teenage life and what to do when the pesky parents and carers were not singing from the same hymn sheet as their children!

Cathy & Claire, of course, weren't real people and the mountains of letters received each day were handled by members of the "Jackie" staff. Despite this gentle deception, the correspondence was always treated with the utmost care and respect. In many cases, those who wrote in felt that they had no one else to turn to.

This was a time when the pages of a magazine were one of the few places where a girl could get meaningful advice, and the "Jackie" staff felt the weight of that responsibility.

Over the years, the problem pages evolved and new experts were found, but the same spirit of support and advice shone through, no matter who was at the helm.

For generations of young women, nothing will ever come close to the sage, thoughtful advice of what they would read in the problem pages of their favourite magazine.

The Cathy 'n' Claire PAGE

Hi there! I'm Cathy

And I'm Claire

If our pictures make us look oh-so-chuffed, they're right — and you must forgive us. The fact is that the Ed (bless his size eight Chelsea boots) has given us a job we're head-over-heels about. Answering problems sent in by you, the readers.

We never thought a room of our own could give us such a kick! And two phones!

All we need is a pile of knotty problems and we'll be in biz. If something's bothering you, why not write to us? Two heads are better than one!

To launch the page, we put our heads together and wrote down all the problems we'd shared with our friends. Was their worry then, your one now?

Here's a selection, and don't forget, let's be hearing from you.

Cathy

And Claire

Dear C. and C.,

My poser? Simple. I want a boy friend. Although I'm considered pretty, fun and sometimes witty, it's no go. I just can't find anyone eligible. Help, please!

Solution? Easy. Get with a swish hairdo and a snazzy dress, slosh on lots of perfume and go where the boys are.

P.S.—Looking appealing will catch him, but it's a girl's charm and lively personality which will really floor an unsuspecting male!

Dear C. and C.,

I love to go on picnics. Thing is, if my boy sees an insect, I practically have to unstick him from the highest branches of the nearest tree.

I'm not a crawlie-lover myself, but this is ridiculous. What can you do with a man like mine?

Colour him yellow!

Dear C. and C.,

My boy friend creates when I tell him I have to be in early on week nights, Dad's orders! What do you think... not... enc...

Dear C. and C.,

We're going Youth-Hostelling this year, but haven't much idea about the average charges.

Youth-Hostelling is fun, exciting and very cheap! Average charges are—each night you stay, 2s-3s according to your age; supper, 2s 6d to 4s; breakfast, 2s 6d; and packed lunch of sandwiches, 1s 6d. If you need to hire a sleeping bag, it costs 1s.

Dear C. and C.,

Liz and I have been pals for years, but now I've a steady boy friend. She feels out of things and hints on joining up with Dave and I in a threesome. What do you think?

Taboo. Instead, why not dig out a spare male and team up as a foursome?

Dear C. and C.,

He's gorgeous—he's super —he's fab! He's the boy I see every morning on the way to work. All he says is a friendly " Hello." How can I get to know him?

Sounds promising. Next time

Dear C. and C.,

Four of us are planning to go to France for our holiday this year. We can all speak fairly good French, but we don't know much about the customs. Can you help? Also, where do we get passports?'

Gee, lucky you! Main thing you'll notice is that the boys are fab, but for more details drop a line to—French Embassy (Tourists' Enquiries), 51 Bedford Square, London, W.C.1.

To get your passport, drop a line or call at your local Ministry of Labour offices.

Dear C. and C.,

My boy friend insists on meeting me inside the pictures, as it saves either of us having to wait around. I'm getting cheesed over this. Can I change him?

Yeah, for another boy! This one's a confirmed meanie. Give him the " So long " line.

Dear C. and C.,

A friend and I have just moved into a flat and want to throw a party next Saturday. There's a boy...

---

the Cathy & Claire

DEAR CATHY & CLAIRE—I'm very worried about my sister who is two years older than me. You see, I think she's been shop lifting and I'm scared she might get into serious trouble. She told me that some of her friends took things from shops regularly.

And one day when I was looking for something in her room, I found an expensive bracelet that I know she couldn't afford to buy.

What can I do to make her see sense before it's too late?

As your sister is older than you, she's bound to resent your interfering in her life. We do agree with you, though, that she's likely to get into serious trouble if you don't do something.

As a start we suggest that you tell her of your suspicions and threaten to tell your parents. This could be the jolt she needs to bring her to her senses.

DEAR CATHY & CLAIRE—I hardly dare tell you my problem—everyone thinks I should be ashamed of it. But still, here goes. I'm fat! Ouch!

I know it's anti-social (I take up one-and-a-half seats on a bus) and could lead to trouble in later life, but really, I can't get worked up about it. Does being fat really matter?

Matter to whom? You say everyone thinks you should be ashamed: do you mean your friends are getting at you to slim? If so, tell them it's none of their business (unless they're sitting next to you on the bus). Or are *you* really worried about your fatness, and just pretending you don't mind?

If you secretly would like to lose weight, stop pretending and do something positive, like going to your doctor and asking for a diet sheet. Then follow it—your nagging friends should be delighted to see you stick to it.

But if you're really resigned to being one of nature's dumplings, take heart—you're probably far more serene than your slender friends who get neurotic if they even smell chips frying. And more clothes shops are catering for supersize girls—though you'll have to face the fact that your clothes will cost more than a skinny Liz's. (Why? Because they take more yardage and more stitching, that's why!)

But paper patterns are cheap enough in all sizes, and it's worth learning to sew if you want a perfect fit and the most up-to-date fashions. You *could* find a dressmaker and have everything made . . . but you said your problem was too much weight, not too much money!

We'd also advise taking up a gentle form of exercise— swimming or dancing, perhaps—to stay in shape. Firm flesh is attractive—floppy flab isn't.

Enjoy yourself. As struggling skinnies, we must admit we envy you. Have a cream bun on us!

Two heads are better than one, they say. That's what we're here for, so why not w... to us? We'll do our best to help you sort out your problems.

Please remember, though, if you want a private reply, to enclose an S.A.E. Our addr... is, Cathy & Claire at "Jackie", 12 Fetter Lane, Fleet Street, London E.C.4. A1B...

DEAR CATHY & CLAIRE—I haven't got a boyfrien... have exams coming up and I have a money problem... thought it would be a good idea to try baby-sitting for s... quiet evenings, and some extra cash, but I don't know h... to go about it. Can you help?

Well, baby-sitting has lots of basic rules. The m... important is that you like babies. We don't just mean t... you go, "Aah, bless him," at baby photos. We mean ... you be calm and comforting when little Tracey or Darr... is yelling with wind; can change nappies without faint... and can pick a baby up without dropping it? If you do... score on any of these, better forget the idea!

Another thing: don't try to get rich too quick. Few you... parents can afford an extra couple of quid for you on ... of the cost of an evening out, and you don't want to pr... yourself out of the market. 15p to 25p an hour is the nor... rate, going up to 25p to 35p after midnight. Decide wha... best for your area, then put a card in a local shop windo... You should do well—good baby-sitters are like gold dust...

More rules: you get yourself to the house—and do arr... on time, in case they've got buses to catch. Make su... you know which room the baby's in (sounds obvious, ... it's no joke opening door after door and maybe wak... other children before you find the right one); where ... bottle is, if it needs one, and where clean nappies a... just in case.

Most children, once in bed, sleep soundly all night, ... never let parents leave without getting the address of ... place they're going to, and the phone number of the chil... doctor. Ten to one you won't need them, but it could ... grim if you did, and hadn't a clue where to find them.

The parents should see you settled in a warm room, w... facilities for making tea or coffee, and biscuits or a sna... You don't have to use them if you don't get hungry ... thirsty, but like the phone numbers, it's better to ha... them than not! When the parents return, the man sho... pay you and see you safely home.

It's easy really. Good luck!

Dear C. and C.,

Can you tell me if there's a holiday resort in Britain with a surplus of males?

Last year, I spent all my money and saw loads of gorgeous girls! Some holiday!

I don't—repeat don't—want to make the same mistake this year.

Only thing we can suggest is a climbing or camping holiday. We don't know many girls brave enough to tackle it. Failing that, if any reader knows a male-mobbed resort, don't be greedy. How about letting us all in on it?

THE CATHY AND CLAIRE PAGE

Dear C. and C.,

My pals say my boy's a cissy, because he's particular about his clothes and the way he speaks.

How can I answer them?

Why should you try? You're his steady. If you think he's O K, forget what other folk say. But if their remarks are making you wonder, you're not keen enough.

Dear C. and C.,

The boy I'm dating now is a bit of a heartbreaker. He tells me his roving days are over and he wants to be my steady. What do you think I should do?

You really like this guy and you know the risk you're running. Take a chance on him.

Dear C. and C.,

I'm in love with a 'way out jazz man who dates me now and then. Trouble is, when I'm with him, I feel more average than 50 per cent. How can I convince him I'm not a turnip head?

Chuck in a few words of the week, for a start. For instance, when you and he are bending an ear to the M.J.Q., tell him it's "tough, mashy, whizzie— —!! the way." You may

CATHY & CLAIRE

We can't promise the but we'll do our best. If y problem and you can't write to us at this addres Jackie, 185 Fleet Street, L Please remember to er

NO SOCIAL LIFE

DEAR CATHY & CLAIRE – We are two girls who have nowhere to go and nothing to do at nights. There are no youth clubs, discos, cafes, etc. round about, and we don't know how to meet any boys. Although there are two boys we fancy, they know this and they haven't done anything about it.

We don't know what to do about this either. We've stayed in playing records till we're sick and tired of it! We were thinking of having a party, but we don't know where to hold one, as our parents won't let us have one in our houses unless one of them stays in. We'd be really grateful if you could suggest a helpful solution. Both of us are 14.

Hopelessly frustrating, isn't it, when you're dying to ... out and meet people and there seems to be ...y!

...'re quite right that a small party — or even ...ended record session — in one of your homes ...d way to get some sort of social scene going. ...ough there seems to be something stopping ...ppening, as well, we reckon that's the very ...hurdle to overcome.

...ur parents insist they're there. Well, perhaps ...such a bad thing for everyone to be aware ...someone responsible in the background. ...that gets out of hand can be a real disaster ... talk to your parents about it, sort out ...ns and theirs, and get something organised ...hose boys you fancy top of the invitation ...

...orrying about what's *not* around in your ... world. Once you start arranging some ...t out of whatever you *have* got, things ...happening!

...ING TO STEAL HIM

...THY & CLAIRE – I have a boyfriend, but ... is my best friend's trying to steal him away ... I don't want to fall out with her, but ... getting me down. Please don't say I ... to her, because I've tried, and she just won't ...

...nderstand how you feel, but if you've ... to your friend and had no success, ... should ask yourself if she really ...friend!

..., try to keep her away from your boy-...er on the evenings when you're not ... Find reasons to go elsewhere ...s to be on the scene when you're ...

...don't want to break with her, but we ...ld let her know that, if you can't rely ...e friend, your friendship can't last. ... hand, we don't believe you should ...h. If your boy really cares for you, ...n't be able to take him from you. ...be swayed by her, well, he really ...much of a loss, can he?

...OKEN DATE

... CLAIRE – I met a boy in the ...; we started talking and he seemed ...e asked me if I'd meet him the next ...

...t he didn't turn up, and I can't ...appened or why he didn't come, ...quite well.

...places he'd be likely to go, and I ...he's never with them, and I can't ...because I'm shy. But I liked him ...like to see him again.

...t to get in touch with this boy ...to take your courage in both ...his friends where you can find him. We think ... you'll find they're quite friendly and willing to help.

But remember, even if you can find ... address, don't expect ... ...missed ...

AWKWARD QUARREL

DEAR CATHY & CLAIRE – The other day I quarrelled with my mum in front of my friend Kay. My mum told me to get out, so I did, and Kay followed me. I stayed in the shed in the back garden for about two hours.

Kay kept me company for a while, then she came back and said she wasn't allowed to come over to my house any more. Evidently her mother had come over to my house to fetch her, and my mum had said she was probably out in the street and it was disgusting. Then, Kay said, my mum slammed the door in her mum's face.

I was going to sleep in the shed, but I got scared and came back and went to bed. In the morning I apologised and my mum said it didn't matter any more, then she told me that I wasn't to go to Kay's house. The thing is that I don't want to drop Kay – she's my best friend and I don't want to find anybody else.

Do you think I should still go around with her and keep it secret? She only lives across the road. I don't know what to do now.

It's awful how storms in teacups can lead to so much bad feeling all round. Your mum's temper was roused and she was all ready to ... anyone's throat — and did so! Now ... just feels embarrassed and wants to ... the whole thing!

It does sound a bit unreasonable to e... give up your best friend, but from her p... she thinks you'll be going over to the ... if you do carry on going around with ...

Well, it's like all quarrels with ... results. They've got to be patched up; a... this case you've managed to do so be... family, now you've got to get togethe... neighbours! Carry on seeing Kay the sa... but don't go to her house for the time be... don't keep it a secret from your mum.

Quarrels have a way of being forgotte... even if the people involved can't be pers... agree immediately. They're at their wo... they're still fresh; so carry on normally... more than likely things will ret... normal in time.

And try not to do anything that'll dis... peace again, right?

HE DOESN'T CALL ME ANY MORE

I've been going out with my boyfriend for three months. I love him very much, and I thought he loved me. But lately he's begun breaking dates with me because he wants to watch television all the time. I don't mind when he says he has to stay in beforehand, but he always says he'll come and collect me, and then he never turns up.

My friend says there's another boy who fancies me, and I'm wondering whether to give up my present boyfriend and see if this boy does want to go out with me.

It certainly sounds high time, you gave things a rest between you and your boy-friend.

You had a good time, enjoyed being together, felt very close to each other. But now — as with lots of relationships till you find a lasting one — things are beginning to fade out. He's not so interested in you; you're quite interested in seeing someone else.

It doesn't have to be a cold, callous break. Discuss it with him, find out what he wants. Perhaps you'll just decide not to go out with one another exclusively for a while, not to expect too much of each other — but still meet on friendly, relaxed terms.

At the moment, though, there are all the signs that it's time to move on.

FLAT VOICE

DEAR CATHY & CLAIRE – My problem is that I have a flat voice. I found this out about two years ago, but now we have three lessons of music a week, all singing.

We have a nice teacher and he is very understanding, but I still find I can't tell him why I don't sing solos when asked to. I want to tell someone, but I don't know how and who to tell, as I find I take quite a long time to trust people and talk to them easily. It's difficult to tell my parents, as I'm away from home, at boarding school.

Please tell me how I can find the courage to tell someone and not worry so much, and sort my problem out.

First of all, remember that a good singing voice is a natural gift. If you don't have one, you don't have one — it just doesn't matter a bit. It's no good at all feeling guilty or embarrassed just because singing isn't one of your talents. There's no doubt you've learn to accept yourself — good and bad!

You sound a bit lonely at school, and we think if you tried to make friends and communicate better with people that'd be an answer to your whole problem.

Since you f...

UNKIND FRIENDS

DEAR CATHY & CLAIRE – My problem is that I don... have many friends, and the friends I do have aren... very nice to me. They push me about and say I'm soft... and then when I try to stand up against them they say... I'm trying to be pushy and leave me on my own.

I have tried to make friends, but I don't seem to fit... in. All this has come as a shock to me, because I... used to have plenty of friends before I went to secondary school.

The girls you've been unfortunate enough to fall in with are hardly worth calling friends, when you come to think about it, are they?

It's very sad that once a group gets an idea you're "easy prey," it's one of the hardest things on earth to put a stop to being pushed around. It's often nothing at all to do with you — in this case it obviously isn't, since you had friends before — it just the situation in which you've found yourself.

The main thing to remember is that the more these girls see they're upsetting you, the more likely they are to go on doing just that. But if you can possibly hide from them just how much they... you, we can assu...

...page

...AR CATHY & CLAIRE – I'm very fond of my boyfrien... ...d everything would be fine between us if we enjoyed ...ng the same things and going to the same places. But ...fortunately we don't and we always end up rowing and ...ver get round to going out at all.

All this is making me very unhappy, and I've been wonder... ...whether I should back down and let him get his own way ...the time. What do you think?

No. We don't think he should be allowed to make all th... ...cisions about going out. You're obviously strong person... ...ties who like to make up your own minds about things ...t you'll have to give a bit if you want to keep going out ...gether.

Perhaps you could try talking things over sensibly when ...u're both in a good mood. If you can't come to some ...rt of satisfactory compromise, and if neither of you can ...nk of things that interest you both, we suggest you take ...ns at chosing where to go and what to do.

...Or you could go out in a crowd and let someone else ...ke the decisions for you.

As the decades went by, some things changed, but some things stayed exactly the same. Fashion, music, work, family, boys... young "Jackie" readers were not short of problems, but luckily there was always wonderful support in the pages of their favourite magazine.

Dear Ellie

Don't suffer in silence. If you've got a problem maybe I can help. Write to me, Ellie, at Jackie, 185 Fleet Street, London EC4A 2HS — with a self-addressed envelope, if you'd like a personal reply.

Recently, I wrote a story and won a competition with it. My teacher told me it was very good and I know it must sound a bit big-headed, but I was pretty pleased with it myself.
Do you know of any addresses where I could be considered for publication in a magazine or book of short stories, particularly for young people?

Congratulations! It's *not* big-headed to take pride in something you've done well. One of the most important things you have to do when it comes to placing a story is to find the right market. Find out which magazines print stories similar to the one you've written, and then submit it, enclosing an SAE for return if it's unsuitable. You'll find the addresses of magazines, publishers, and their requirements in a reference book called 'The Writers' and Artists' Year Book', which you'll find in your local reference library. It's also packed full of useful information for any budding writer. So — look out Jeffrey Archer!

I'm nearly 16 and very unhappy because I'm flat-chested. All my friends wear bras. I recently started my periods. Does that mean I'm going to stop growing now and stay flat-chested for ever?

No, it doesn't mean that, so stop worrying! You're going to continue to develop. It's a long process, and it doesn't run to a strict timetable. Lots of girls worry at this stage of their development either because they think their bust is too small — or too large. If you'd like a leaflet, entitled 'Body Talk', write enclosing an SAE and I'll put one in the post to you. It should reassure you that you're just the same as the rest of us!

I'm 15 and I've been grounded because I got involved with a boy my parents don't like. They said I wasn't to see him any more, but I did, so they've stopped me going out at all, even with my friends. I still want to see him though, and they can't keep me in for ever.

Parents can sometimes forget how unfair their own mum and dad could seem when they were younger. Try jogging their memories by casually questioning them about their younger days — it might help! Then if you're still convinced they're being unreasonable, find out if they'll compromise by meeting him again now their tempers have cooled, and give him another chance.

But first, ask yourself if this boy seems more attractive to you, just because your parents don't like him.

I'm crazy about my boyfriend and we spend a lot of time together. Sometimes, though, we have a fight and I start crying because I'm really scared we'll split up. My boyfriend says I'm being stupid and that I should trust him, but I can't help feeling this way. He's really important to me.

I know he's important, but if you put a lot of pressure on him like this, you're going to scare him off. Most boys don't like emotional scenes. They get scared, and a bit embarrassed and who could blame them! If you want to hold on to him, give him a little room to breathe. If things are going well just now, why torture yourself imagining you're going to break up? And even if you did break up, you'd discover that, just like a lot of other girls, you'd cope. It's not the end of the world.

I'm 16, short, fat, hairy, spotty and ugly. I've never had a boyfriend and I have no pals. My life at home is misery — I'm not what Mum wanted. My cousins are tall, slim and beautiful and two of them are models.

You can't help being 16 and short, but you can certainly start putting everything else to rights. Cut down on greasy, highly spiced and fatty foods, decide on a de-fuzzing method which suits you — either cream remover or safety razors and get advice on skin care. There are Jackie leaflets to cover all these problems available if you send in an SAE. Once you've taken your appearance in hand, your confidence should have a much-needed boost. Then you can start going to clubs, or take up a sport, or some other hobby to get you out and meeting people. You're not a helpless victim, it's up to you to make the most of yourself and your opportunities. Few of us are *born* beautiful and popular, we've got to work at it!

Try to stop feeling sorry for yourself, and be constructive about your problems. I'm pretty sure you're wrong about your mum too — why not ask her?

I've been promised a horse of my own and Dad's started to build a stable for it. My dad is a landscape gardener and his only day off is a Sunday and although work has started on the stable, it's kind of petered out. I don't want to nag him because I know he gets tired — but I'm so desperate to get my horse. He's said he'll get someone in to lay bricks for him, but nothing's happened yet. Mum says not to pester him and I do try but I get so impatient.

Be careful not to sound like a record that's stuck. Nagging only makes people impatient with you. It helps if you show willing to do your bit, whether it's helping to save up towards the cost, or doing extra work. Offer to help — whether it's with the nice clean end like planning or designing, or with the more messy (and probably more fun) building, mixing cement and laying bricks. And remember your mum probably knows the best way to handle your dad here, so get her on your side to put in a word.

I'm really worried because I started my periods three months ago and I haven't had one for 55 days. I'm too shy to talk to anybody.

That's a pity because you could have been spared all this anxiety. You would have found out that this is not an uncommon thing to happen — periods can take quite a time to settle into a regular rhythm. Your embarrassment is understandable, but it's not necessary.

The best thing you can do is stop worrying — being anxious can actually delay the start of a period, so just do your best to forget all about it and let things happen naturally!

Help! I've got mock exam and then my 'O' grades. I top class but the work is getting on top of me. I ca seem to do any real stud till the week before exa start, even though I kno that's too late. If I try, m wanders or I begin to f sleepy. My parents are expecting a lot of me, they don't push me. I w like to let them down.

You can do a lot t yourself. Get hold of boo papers and set yourself a to answer a certain num questions. That will add pressure and excitemen to get down to work. St friends often helps, too surprisingly enough. O revision schedule with together you should m stick to it. Finally, start about not letting yours you'll only do well if yo exams are important luck!

A month ago we girl to stay with exchange sche was very happy here and I dev crush on her. S now and she's long letter an miss her. I wr but I didn't te I'm usually s lucky person just now. Is i to feel like t

It's a stage y through and it's not abnormal. N like this over a b but never thou this over anoth your crush is ju liking, admirin like someone. out your feeli make your fri Just enjoy yo start saving t next year. Th feel better.

Dear t

The Royal National Institute for the [
Information Dept.,
105 Gower Street,
London WC1A 6AH.

The RNID also publish two book which may help you teach yourself s language — called 'Sign and Say' b One and Two they cost £1.50 each, the same address.

I am 14 and have been g out with boys since I was 1 My eldest sister is 16 and h only just started going out w boys. She keeps telling me should wait till I am her age now I don't know whether t stop seeing my boyfriend o not.

If you're happy with your relation with boys then I don't see why you s change. Perhaps your sister just had met anyone she liked enough to go o with until now — there isn't an 'ideal' to start going out with boys.

The relationships you have at 16 probably be a bit more serious than ones you have at the moment, just a probably notice a difference now fro those you had when you were 10! S don't let what your sister does influe you too much — do what you feel is for *you*.

I am 15 and have never been out with a boy. I've fancied a boy in the year ab me for ages, and my friend have asked him out for me he won't go. People tell me look for someone else and tried, but I can't forget abo him. I get so depressed ab

I fancy this boy who's 15 I'm 14. I asked him out but said 'No' though his family s he likes me a lot. I asked hi he liked me and he said he

Recently my mate had an idea that we should write a poison pen letter. I took her seriously and I sent two. The teacher found out and had a word with the class and said if she found out who did it she'd take them to a child doctor. I didn't know it was such a serious thing. I don't want anyone to know I did this, and besides, it's my mate's fault too. Don't tell me to tell anyone as I don't want to get into trouble.

...ing nasty anonymous letters may ...nny, but they're anything but ... the people who receive them. I ... *do* realise now what a spiteful ...ghtless thing you've done and ...re not just sorry because these ...ve been reported.

Dear E

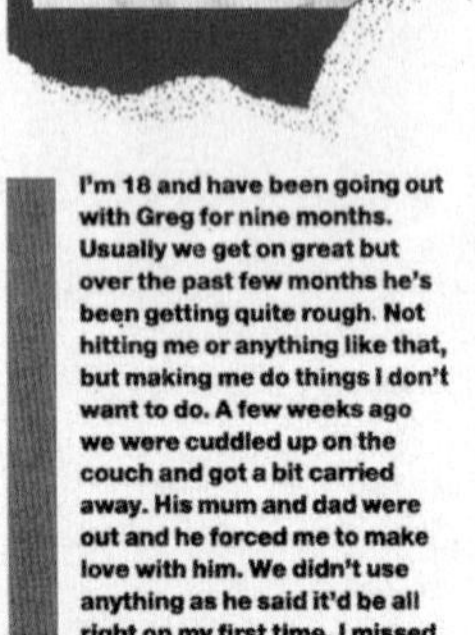

counsellor so why not confide i them to begin with? Alternative you could get in touch with the Pregnancy Advisory Service, 1 13 Charlotte Street, London W Tel. 01 637 8962 who'll give yo lots of invaluable advice and support.

There is a way to get throug this so start making the first mo now — after the initial shock ha worn off you could be surprise how much back-up and help y family can offer. I do hope everything works out OK for yo and wish you lots of luck.

I'm 18 and have been going out with Greg for nine months. Usually we get on great but over the past few months he's been getting quite rough. Not hitting me or anything like that, but making me do things I don't want to do. A few weeks ago we were cuddled up on the couch and got a bit carried away. His mum and dad were out and he forced me to make love with him. We didn't use anything as he said it'd be all right on my first time. I missed my next period and have just had the results of a pregnancy test — positive. I'm at my wits' end about what to do. I live away from home so I can't talk to my mum. I only have a few months left to do at college and I haven't told Greg as I'm scared of how he'll react. I can't bear thinking about abortion and I really can't see any way to turn. Everything's such a mess.

I sympathise with how you feel but this isn't something that's going to sort itself out on its own. You're going to need a lot of help and support but it's up to you to face this responsibility and start dealing with it. I'd think very carefully about Greg's involvement in all this — if he's not treating you well now, chances are things will

I'm 14 and I know this boy who's 19. He always dance with me at discos and he's very first boy who's kissed I'm really shy and a bit frightened of him. He alway tries it on and I can't get aw from him as he holds me so tightly. The last time he trie put his hand down my blous and I don't feel ready for anything like that yet. I don like him much but I can't te him to go away as he'd only laugh at me.

So what? Let him laugh — better than being groped by a g you don't even like! Let him kno you're not interested and be fir about it. This type of guy is obviously pretty insensitive, so feelings aren't worth concernin yourself over, after all, he doesn consider yours, does he? Ther absolutely no need to feel frightened or pressured. If you you can't cope alone or he wo take no for an answer, enlist th help of an older relative or your parents. Next time you're at a disco just ignore him complete and refuse to dance with him. Once he sees you're no longer going to be intimidated he shou soon get the message and leav you alone.

I'm 13 years old and starte periods about a year ago. I' read in books that you get a

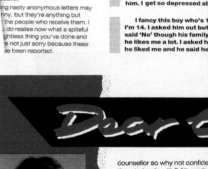

llie

If you've been flicking through the magazine looking for 'Cathy & Claire' then you're probably a bit surprised to see a new-look Problem Page with my face at the top! After many years of solving your problems, Cathy and Claire have moved on, and from now on I'll be here to help you out so if you need advice or just want a shoulde to cry on, write to me, marking your letter 'Dear Ellie', at Jackie, 185 Fleet Street, London EC4A 2HS.

If you'd like a personal reply please remember to enclose an SAE — if you dor then bear in mind that there may not be r for me to print a reply on this page in tim help you.

I am so upset, sometimes I wish I was dead. My dad has been put in prison for two years, and my mum is cracking up, she just sits and cries all the time. I've had to go on free meals at school because we have no money now, and all my friends have stopped speaking to me, except to call me names. I am not allowed to see my dad and I miss him so much, but my mum will not mention his name. Sometimes I think I'm going mad, it's all too much.

You must remember that none of this our fault. Your 'friends' are being orant and cruel when you need their pport more than ever. Is there a cher you trust that you can talk to? I k it's time someone at school spoke hese people on your behalf, and for r own good.

Your life has obviously been terribly upted and I think your mum will need of support, too. Perhaps together could contact one of the following ups who help people in your situation lose an SAE if you write to them):-

oners Wives & Families Soc.,
Caledonian Road,
don W1
278 3981)
ow (Help and Service for Offenders' es)
nslow Road,
thampton,
2 OJD
3) 2298 359

If you need someone to chat to in fidence yourself, contact
PCAS
National Assoc. of Young People's nselling & Advice Services)
23 Albion Street,
estershire.
6GD
3) 554775
Good luck!

people, rather than listen to gossi have been given the impression t relationship will bring surprises — nasty ones. Take things slowly, fi about him, what he's like, and if I you well, before you get too invo

I'm 12, have starte periods and have begu develop. Now a boy at has asked me to go ou him, but I don't know to or not. I'm scared h out about me and tell

When you have a bust, pe see that you do, so what's the No-one need know you have though. Anyway, growing up be ashamed of — boys chan can be just as self-conscious girls.

Don't be embarrassed a body — physical changes n you. Lots of girls your age w for them! If the idea of starti with boys is a bit too much handle at the moment, or y this particular boy, you dor 'yes'. It's up to you to deci are ready.

My problem is known my best fr a year and when

Dear Ellie

I really hate the school where I've been for six weeks. I'm not lazy — I like my subjects, but something about the place irritates me. Don't tell me things will get better because people keep saying that and it's not true. I really want a tutor at home, but my parents say they wouldn't be able to afford it. I actually tried running away, but they still make me go to school.

OK — imagine you got what you think you want — a home tutor. I think after a while you'd get more irritated with that situation, being stuck at home studying, missing out on friends, break times or different teachers to make the day more interesting!

You say you hate school, but you can't specify why. Your newness could be what unsettles you, not the actual place. But things won't improve if you're pessimistic. Six weeks is nowhere near long enough to know what somewhere new's really like.

You enjoy your subjects, so that's a good start. Be determined to prove yourself wrong about your first impressions. Be friendly and do your best at lessons, then you're more likely to find out your school's not as bad as you thought.

I used to be really cheerful and happy, I was quite popular and had lots of hobbies. Now I've got a boring, lonely life and I'm fed up. I can't put any effort into anything any more and I've lost interest in all the hobbies I loved. My friends and family all seem awkward and difficult and I always seem to be involved in scenes. It's like there's a devil inside me and I can't control it.

What *is* inside you is a mixture of moods that go up and down without any explanation. Combine this with the personality clashes and changing interests you're experiencing and you get something known as growing up! It's a time when it's unusual *not* to feel unsettled, due to all the changes in your body taking place, so it's not the people you know who seem awkward, it's you!

But don't fret over this awkward phase, everything will fall into place, but just knowing what's going on should help you, as will admitting to your family when you feel down — they'll understand, they'll have been through the same thing too.

Don't let depression drag you down — take that first step in making yourself feel better by writing to me at Dear Ellie, Jackie, 185 Fleet Street, London, EC4A 2HS — with a self-addressed envelope, if you'd like a personal reply.

My boyfriend has just chucked me for no reason at all. I'd been going out with him for six months and I ended up sleeping with him. I cry myself to sleep every night because I can't believe he doesn't want me. I feel dirty and used and everything's gone wrong since he left me. I can't get on with my parents, or do anything right at school. No one cares what happens to me.

It's always tough to be dropped, especially when you feel used too, as you do. I bet lots of readers who've felt the same sympathise with you and would tell you that the hurt you feel will fade, given time. It can be hard to keep feelings under control but because relationships are often brief and breezy at this stage it is a good idea to build up any deep commitments slowly. You can only feel used if you let it happen, remember, so next time you get involved with a boy (which you will, I promise), think back to this experience and learn from it.

And stop thinking people don't care about you — of course they do! But you should care too, so look after yourself, forget feeling bad, let your hurt heal and start looking forward to the future.

I'm 14 and fancy a boy in my class. He's really nice and we get on well. The other day we were alone in the classroom and he asked me out. I asked him if he really meant it and he then said he was only joking. That really upset me because I like him a lot.

He probably had to pluck up a lot of courage to ask you out and if he wasn't sincere, surely he wouldn't have asked you when you were both alone?

I think your reply knocked his confidence a bit. He could have been expecting a refusal so he fibbed to save face . . . It's up to you now to continue where he left off. Choose a moment when you can mention casually you'd really like to go out with him. You could even send a subtle message.

I bet he'll be glad you made the second move, and that you feel the same way he does!

I'm 14, with a sister and brother who are both married and each have two children. When they come to visit us, I feel very jealous and start being mean to all of them — just because they have children and I don't. One day I'd like to have five of my own. My mum always asks me to play with the kids but I don't because it annoys me that my mum treats me as one of them. I can't help wishing they were mine but they're not and because of this I ... rotten ...

I'm 15 and have a 12-year-old sister who won't leave my things alone. She looks in my diary and reads my letters. She even tells other people what's in them. I tried talking to her, but we ended up screaming at each other. Eventually, I told my parents and they spoke to her. But she's still at it and my mum is now reading them, too! All this is making me moody and that's also getting me in trouble with my mum and dad.

It's understand... upse...

My friends have fallen out with me over something ... I've tri...

... caught me smoking ... mates and since then ... een really nasty. I cry a ... use I'm scared she'll ... ad. I've tried to give it ... can't. I'm 13.

By writing to me ... he first step ...

llie

Don't lose sleep over a worry or problem, maybe I can help? I'll certainly try. Write to me, Ellie, at Jackie, 185 Fleet Street, London E... 2HS. If you'd like personal or urge reply, don't forge enclose a stampe addressed envelo I can write back.

t if it's exceptionally heavy, ong smelling or uncomfortable it uld be that you've picked up a d infection. It can be easily eated by your doctor so go along d have a check-up. There's ally no need to feel shy or barrassed — they deal with rsonal things like this every day, at's what they're there for. It's ally not very healthy to wear npons every day and it certainly ouldn't be necessary. Some s find it reassuring to wear ni-towels or liners just for shness on the days when charge increases, but they ouldn't be needed every day of e month. I'm sure your doctor l be able to reassure you and t your mind at rest over this, so e sooner you go along, the oner you can start getting on h your life normally.

I'm 13 and my chest is still as flat as a pancake! Obviously, I don't wear a bra and when I get changed for P.E. I know everyone laughs and smirks. I haven't started my periods yet either and I feel so left out. Mum keeps asking if I need any towels, but I know she wouldn't understand how stupid and freaky I feel. I share a room with my older sister and even she laughs at my figure. It really hurts my feelings when people laugh and I've even stopped going out so much because I'm so self-conscious.

Believe it or not, I get loads of ters just like yours so please n't think you're alone in feeling e this. I know it's hard when all ur friends seem to be way ahead you but believe me, you'll soon tch up. Every girl has their own ological clock and although me may be slower than others begin with, things even emselves out eventually. If your ends laugh at you, they're not ally the type of friends worth ving anyway, are they? They ay be mature in their bodies but eir minds certainly have a lot of owing up to do.

conscious about wearing a and you'll look pretty trendy same time. Try not to worry much. Honest, in a few year you'll be wondering what all fuss was about!

I recently started going o with this boy called Barry. really nice to me but the trouble is I can't seem to s being horrible to him. He k on giving me little present I'm scared he'll think I'm ju using him. I don't know wh feel like this. Is it just becau of my age?

It could be. When you're you it's easy to fall in and out of love pretty quickly and it's not unusua to feel a bit mixed up sometimes. get the feeling that perhaps Barry is a little more serious about this relationship than you are and I think you should try to set things straight before things go any further. Try to explain to Barry that you don't really need presents and that although you appreciate the thought, it makes you feel uncomfortable.

From the sounds of things I suspect you'd be happier if you cooled things off a bit and got a bit more breathing space. Try to concentrate less on the 'romantic love' aspect and more on just building up a comfortable friendship. You're not using anybody if you're honest and straightforward about your feelings, so don't feel pressured by guilt in any way.

Bros Fan from Glasgow.

It sounds as if Paul is genuinely sorry. Why not give him the chance to explain and then take things from there? Once you know the full story you'll be better able to sort

talk it over

PROBLEMS PROBLEMS PROBLEMS

Don't let a problem get you down — why not share it with me instead? Write to Maria at Jackie Magazine, 185 Fleet Street, London EC4A 2HS — and I'll do all I can to help.

If you'd like a

ANSWERS PLEASE

I'm 14 years old and have two questions which are worrying me. The first question is, I started my periods just over a year ago and still get a discharge — is this normal? The second question is, can you catch AIDS from kissing?

Well, since your questions seem totally unrelated I'll deal with them separately.

It is normal to continue to experience a discharge once your periods have started but some people find it heavier or more noticeable than others. You need only worry if a discharge becomes discoloured or has a smell, as this could indicate a slight infection such as thrush.

Your second question is a little less straightforward to answer. The chances of catching HIV, the virus which leads to AIDS, through kissing are almost negligible but technically, I suppose it is possible. The HIV virus is transmitted through the exchange of body fluids such as saliva or blood, but unless you have an open cut or ulcer inside your mouth and are kissing an infected partner there really is no danger.

It's sensible to be aware of the risk of AIDS these days but it's also important to get the facts straight in order to avoid unnecessary worry. Your local health centre should have a range of free leaflets to help explain things in more detail, or you can contact:

The Terrence Higgins Trust,
52-54 Grays Inn Road,
London,
WC1X 8JU.
Tel. 071 242 1010 (daily, 3 pm-10 pm).

OUT OF TOUCH

For three years me and this other girl were inseparable friends. We lost ... when we

I don't think, in fairness, that you can expect this girl to be your best friend again just because you're back in the same class. You'll both have changed after all this time, and it follows that you'll both have made some other, new friends. You can't recapture the past, so instead of feeling sad when you think about your old friendship try to be more positive and look on it as a fond memory.

I don't see any harm in being friendly towards this girl now but it's unrealistic to want her to give up her new friend in favour of you. I get the impression that you may be feeling a bit lonely yourself and, if that's the case, the answer really is to try to get more involved with other people.

Maybe this girl will be happy to have you as one of her friends, but you should try developing new friendships, too. I hope things work out OK.

BULLYING BLUES

I'm 15 years old and being bullied at school. It's been going on now for over four years and, although I've tried everything I can think of to stop it, nothing helps. I don't have any real friends who could back me up and I can't talk to a Guidance teacher at school as they're always too busy or wouldn't believe me. I cry myself to sleep every night and just feel like killing myself. Please help.

"I'm being bullied at school."

Being bullied isn't easy to cope with, I know, and I understand how depressed all this must be making you. Bullies thrive on being able to scare and intimidate people, so trying to deal with things yourself isn't always the answer.

You must speak up about ... can get the

teacher can offer, I'm sure it'd be a great relief for you just to be able to talk about what's happening.

These bullies must be exposed so they can't go on intimidating you — once they see you're prepared to stand up to them their 'game' won't seem much fun any more. I hope this gives you a starting point anyway.

TAMPON TROUBLE

I've recently started using tampons and, although I don't have any trouble inserting them, I do have another problem. After wearing one for a while, I feel as if it's slipping down, making me very uncomfortable. I'm sure I'm putting them in properly to begin with so why does this happen? I've tried different brands but still have the same problem.

Well, once a tampon's inserted properly, you shouldn't be able to feel it at all and it certainly shouldn't feel as if it's falling out. My guess is that you may not be inserting it far enough up, or else you're using a size that's too large.

Try switching to a smaller size and ensure you change tampons at least every four hours. With a bit of practice I'm sure you'll be able to overcome any worries — it's really just a case of developing your confidence and finding out what's right for you.

IN A SWEAT

I'm nearly 10 years old and have a problem with sweating. I never used to be bothered but recently I've noticed that I sweat a lot and I'm too embarrassed to talk to my mum. Please print this and give me some advice.

All that's happening is that ... starting to grow up

MAGICAL *Memories*

WHAT is "Jackie"? The most obvious answer, of course, is that it was a phenomenally popular magazine. You could also call it the voice of a generation – more than one in fact – and a friend and confidante to millions of girls.

But what made "Jackie" such an important part of growing up for so many?

There are many possible answers to this question, too, but if we are to distil it down to one thing, it is the passion and enthusiasm of the many journalists, designers and editors who worked on the magazine over the years.

Over the next few pages, we go behind the scenes at "Jackie".

We find out what it was like creating the weekly magic that was every issue of the magazine, and we meet just some of the dedicated people who worked to ensure every word and image published meant something to the young audience.

Of course, working on a magazine like "Jackie" was hard graft, but there was plenty of fun to be had too.

Turn over to hear more about the staff's hair-spray and pop music infused adventures!

Introducing... The Jackie

Cover Girl!

The snap-shot that started it all — Nikki's winning photo!

Nikki arrives in London — can you tell her knees are shaking?

This one . . .

. . . or this one?

Cover G

Remember our Jackie Cover Girl competition held 'way back in March, when the search was on — the search for a Jackie reader to appear on our cover? After sifting through thousands of entries — with much debating, squabbling and scratching of heads — we finally decided on a winner.

We chose fourteen-year-old Nikki Channon from Bristol — and for the story of her super stay in London, read on!

Nikki arrived — slightly nervous, she confessed! — in London after travelling from Bristol by train, courtesy of British Rail, who arranged her Golden Rail weekend in London. After being met by Liz, our fashion assistant, Nikki was whisked off for a meal — followed by a good night's sleep at the Royal Kensington Hotel, as there was a busy day ahead tomorrow!

Bright and early next morning, Nikki was taken to the head office of Naughty! clothing — the super sportswear people — and presented with a £100 voucher to spend on Naughty! clothes, which was part of her super prize. Ever been spoilt for choice? Nikki certainly was, and after much "Which one should I choose? D'you like this colour?" she emerged clutching bulging bags of clothes — her only worry being how she'd fit them all in her wardrobe!

Naughty's head office is the place where many of their clothes are designed, and Nikki was so intrigued by what went on behind the scenes that she's planning a return visit to find out a lot more about what's involved in designing clothes.

Next on the agenda was the British Shoe Corporation in New Bond Street to browse round the fantastic footwear! At British Shoe, Nikki was given her £50 voucher — yet another part of her prize! — and let loose to pick, choose and try on whatever caught her eye. Then, after a snatched lunch, it was off to the photographer's studio for Nikki's first-ever photo session!

Make-up artist Francine, from Miners, chatted to Nikki about how she liked to look, before applying a light base of Bare Make-Up in Medium. To add shape to Nikki's face, she gently brushed Double Blush in Rainbow Blush along Nikki's cheeks. Eyes were coloured with Pearls from the Pot of Gold Collection, and finished with two coats of All Weath... ara in Browny Black. Nikki's lip... mixture of Moisture Rich ... Pearl Flutter, and her nails ... Shield Nail Colour, also in ... r from Jingles then styled ... ousse for extra body and ... for added fullness. ... her star-treatment make- ... brighter when a couple of ... udio — Michael J. Mullins ... rn Romance! ...roan!), they whisked Nikki ... and one thing was sure ...rt!

Try this for size!

Yes — red's definitely Nikki's colour!

Am I imagining all this?

Being a celebrity's thirsty work!

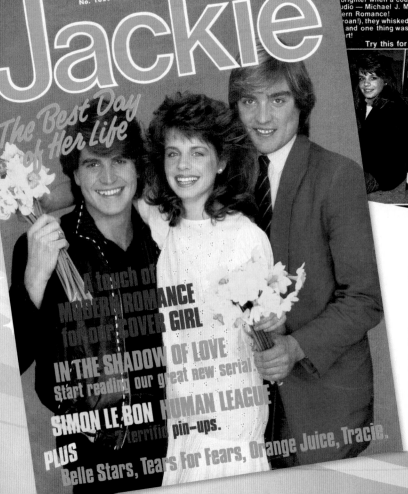

Jackie
The Best Day of Her Life
No. 1020 JULY 23, 1983 — THURSDAYS 18p IR 26p (inc. VAT)

A touch of MODERN ROMANCE for our COVER GIRL
IN THE SHADOW OF LOVE Start reading our great new serial!
SIMON LE BON HUMAN LEAGUE Terrific pin-ups.
PLUS Belle Stars, Tears For Fears, Orange Juice, Tracie.

Q TELL US ABOUT ENTERING THE MODELLING COMPETITION.

A I was recalling when I took the phone call to say I'd won the competition, which was confusing as I didn't actually enter — my big sister entered me but didn't tell me! "Jackie" magazine told me that part of my prize was to meet and have my photograph taken with my favourite pop star. They were a bit hesitant when I told them it was Michael Jackson and said, "Um, we think he might be a bit busy. Do you like Modern Romance?"

I Was A Jackie Cover Star!

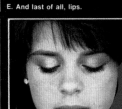

B. Foundation comes first . . .

C. . . . then it's on to the eyes.

D. Getting cheeky with blusher!

E. And last of all, lips.

Nikki looked ... before we got to work on her!

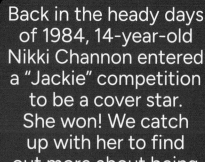

Back in the heady days of 1984, 14-year-old Nikki Channon entered a "Jackie" competition to be a cover star. She won! We catch up with her to find out more about being a "Jackie" girl.

– looking gorgeous!

The Runners-Up!

Meet our two runners-up — Michelle Evans from Surrey, and Sarah Chapman from Southampton. Both girls won a super Miner's Make-Up Kit, and a £25 voucher to spend at any branch of Saxone, Dolics, Trueform or Lilley & Skinner.

Nikki has modelled for Essentials magazine.

Q DID YOU ALWAYS READ "JACKIE"?

A Always!

Q WHAT WERE YOUR FAVOURITE BITS?

A The photo stories were fab! Loved the tips on how to apply make-up and the problem page was always fun!

Q WHICH POSTERS WERE ON YOUR BEDROOM WALL BACK THEN?

A Duran Duran, Spandau Ballet and Haircut 100.

Q WHAT HAVE YOU DONE SINCE THEN?

A How long have you got?! I worked in graphic design, advertising, PR and corporate hospitality. Then I went on to be a singer for about 10 years which is how I met my husband Jay. When it was time to hang up our microphones in 2008 we applied and featured on "Escape To The Country". We found our home and moved to Wales to pursue our dream of running holiday accommodation. We renovated three holiday cottages and our own beautiful home, and set up two businesses, www.brechfaforestbarns.co.uk (totally dog friendly holiday cottages) and www.mudtrek.com (fully catered, guided mountain bike breaks). "Escape to the Country" came back to feature us on "I Escaped to the Country" in 2017. We're so proud of our achievements but every good book needs a new chapter, so we are selling up to move to Andalucia with our two beagles Alfie and Dilly. Oh, and now I'm 55 I might try my luck to become a cover girl for "Saga" magazine!

Q WILL YOU ALWAYS BE A "JACKIE" GIRL?

A Once a "Jackie" girl, always a "Jackie" girl!

Images: Courtesy of Nikki Channon

WORK IT

SHAHEENA DAVD AND PAULINE BELL JOINED THE JACKIE STAFF FOR A DAY AND FOUND OUT WHAT IT'S LIKE TO BE *JOURNALISTS*.

WHEN Shaheena and Pauline arrived in our hall they were shaking with anticipation (or was it fear?). We had a lot in store for them.

The first thing we did in the office was find them desks. Once they sat down they settled in to the chaotic atmosphere really quickly but they did get a little snowed under with "galleys". They're the form our features take after they've been typewritten and before they reach the page. Usually, there are lots of mistakes on them that we have to correct. Shaheena and Pauline took to the concept of galley-corring like ducks to water and twenty minutes (and three bottles of Tipp-Ex) later they were mistake-free!

As they were so sickeningly good at that and were beginning to show us up we let loose with the dreaded "junior duties"!! Ha-ha — that'd teach them!

First off we deluged them with some of the letters — we receive about two hundred a day — so we got them to sift through them, sorting out the competition entries from the letters for Graham's page! About half an hour later they emerged bleary-eyed and never wishing to see a first class stamp again in their lives! However, there's no rest for the wicked (or something) so we dragged them screaming towards the typewriter to type our hand-written copies! This is no mean task!

"Get down to the canteen and get it right this time!"

"Hello, is that Lorraine from Five Star?"

CANTEEN CALL!

When, at last, we could stand the "stunning" pace of Pauline's typing no more we turned our attention to Shaheena. Yep, it was her turn to suffer!

In the office we pin up all of our front covers on the wall — high up on the wall and, you guessed it, Shaheena had to scale the dizzy heights (without a net) and pin it up! After suffering a severe attack of vertigo we let her come back down to earth . . . only to face yet another ordeal . . . the canteen call!

Both Shaheena and Pauline were given strict orders — five coffees (two black, two white, one brown), three teas (all black) and "numerous" packets of crisps. But what did they go and do? Get it all wrong of course! Not only did they mix up the beverages but they forgot the crisps! What is the world coming to? Once we'd sorted out that little misdemeanour we decided they'd had enough of the cruel jibes and settled them down to "real work" . . .

First of all we introduced them to Pauline (another one) our "princess of pop" who "ran through" the week's new releases with them, forecasting the "hits" and the "misses". Suitably impressed, Shaheena and Pauline had a rake around Pauline's desk, looking at the advance copies of albums and singles, but alas, there were no spanking new Brother Beyond or Michael Jackson goodies to be had! Sniffling just a little, we passed them over to the Graham you know and love who was ready with a caring word and a dry shoulder. Graham, the true professional showed them how he decided what letters to include in his page (basically the ones that are nice to him!). Shaheena and Pauline were obviously enthralled because at the slightest hint of our bookful of male models they were over like a shot to our beauty files! Once they'd scrambled through the books, arguing about each and every hunk and looking desperately for their phone numbers!

INTERVIEWING FIVE STAR!

It was then that we sprung our surprise on them . . . That morning Pauline, the Pop Ed, had arranged to do a phone interview (or a "phoner") with the Fives they call Star, yes, Five Star, and Shaheena and Pauline were to be the two lucky people who'd interview the megastar that is Lorraine Pearson!

After picking Shaheena and Pauline off the floor, we sat them at the phone and told them to do their worst — we wanted the gossip and, if possible, an exclusive exposé! They found out loads — who their fave TV presenter was, whether or not they watched 'Neighbours' and how many cars they had. However, we didn't find out if Lorraine and Eddie Murphy had really been an "item" or, indeed, if they still were!

The interview finished and their copy beautifully written and typed we mulled over their "fun-packed" visit. They'd had a busy afternoon, tackling most of the jobs in the office and doing them all pretty darned well too, but what did they think?

Pauline; "It's been really exciting and I'd love to work here all the time. You must have a great laugh!"

Shaheena; "I've had a really good time — the only thing is — I'll have to write a report about it in school. Can I take one of your male model books for inspiration?"

With that we plied Shaheena and Pauline with lots of pressies and bade them a fond farewell!

YOU SHOULD BE A JOURNALIST IF . . .

- You're creative
- You're able to work under pressure and to a deadline
- You like meeting people
- You're well organised
- You don't mind constructive criticism
- You enjoy seeing your work in print

OUT!

Pauline tries to decipher the handwriting!

Graham (alias "Santa") with two of his elves.

The Pop Ed "runs down" the chart.

Shaheena reaches the top!

Pauline and Shaheena go mad with the Tipp-Ex. Cheeky young scamps!

"He's the nicest." "No, he is!"

YOU SHOULDN'T BE A JOURNALIST IF . . .

- You hate sitting all day
- It takes you half an hour to think of one sentence
- You find it difficult to express yourself
- You're unimaginative
- You're shy with people or on the phone
- You're scatter-brained and forget things easily

FOR MORE INFORMATION

The best way to get into journalism is to write to the publishing companies and magazines themselves. Write a chatty letter about yourself, your hobbies and interests and, of course, your qualifications.

You'll need at least a 'B' grade in Higher or A-Level English and, of course, your spelling and grammar will need to be good.

Some colleges run journalism courses that will teach you the full range of the job, including typing, shorthand and public speaking.

When writing to any publication or college for information, don't forget to enclose an S.A.E.

Hi!

Wendy

Memories Of A
Jac

For many young journalists, "Jackie" Magazine provided two things: the best training you could possible imagine – and loads of fun! Wendy Rigg was one such wide-eyed, enthusiastic budding writer. . .

CONSIDER myself extremely lucky to have had the chance to work on my favourite magazine, and to be asked to appear on the front cover. I was seventeen years old, and fresh out of school, when I started as a trainee journalist at DC Thomson in Dundee.

It was 1975, and my dad had seen the job advert in the local paper.

I applied and had no idea that it would eventually lead to a job as Editorial Assistant at "Jackie".

As a reader I pored over the fashion pages and loved those long-legged, doe-eyed illustrations by artist Jil Shipley – they were my favourite pages. I copied those illustrations at school and doodled them in art class when I should have been concentrating on drawing the still life set-up – oranges, grapes, an apple, a loaf of bread and a Mateus Rose wine bottle – much to the annoyance of the bearded, kilted art teacher.

After a few months working on the newspaper, "The Courier", I was transferred to "Jackie".

I got the bus to work every day from home in a little village called Dairsie, in Fife, and had a mile-long walk up a country road. Still, I made a big effort in all weathers including snow and frost with my outfits. I knitted elbow-length fingerless gloves, and made or customised my clothes, as well as wearing things I found in vintage

shops in the Grassmarket or Stockbridge in Edinburgh, or Dens Road Market in Dundee. Net curtains twitched in the village as I stalked my way to the bus stop in my four-inch-heeled Chelsea Cobbler lace-up ankle boots, Victorian white petticoats and home-made poncho.

My colleagues at "Jackie" were a friendly bunch, but I still felt like a naïve schoolgirl. Desks were piled high with all manner of papers, press releases, typed-up features and illustrations. Nina Myskow, the Editor, was the only person with a phone, and the rest of us had to book time to use one in a cubicle, in the afternoons only. The operator had to connect you, and if you were on too long she'd cut you off.

My enthusiasm for fashion led to me assisting the Fashion and Beauty Editor, Alison Plummer, and when Nina asked me to accompany Alison to London to assist on fashion and cover shoots, I jumped at the chance.

We went to a studio on Portobello Road,

No. 651 JUNE 26 1976 THURSDAY □6p

Jackie
KEEPS ON ROLLING!

DISASTER-I'VE DONE IT AGAIN!
HOW TO GET YOUR FOOT OUT OF YOUR MOUTH!

HOT FAVOURITES
SIZZLING SUMMER FASHIONS TO KEEP YOU COOL

GREAT NEW ROLLERS

Jackie Girl 70s

where we worked with photographer Susan Mayer, and the "it models" of the time – girls like Lesley Ash, Jo Wood and Vivienne Lynn. I was photographed in dungarees with roller skates on, and can you imagine how I felt when the picture ended up on the front cover of the magazine in June, 1976? It was an amazing feeling going down to the print room to collect the first editions, and seeing my face on hundreds of thousands of copies of "Jackie". Honestly, I couldn't quite believe it. I had to keep going into the newsagents to look at it.

I went on to appear on more covers and annuals over the next couple of years. I often modelled the knitting patterns – leg warmers, a tabard, mitts on strings. We had a fantastic designer, Alan Dart, who created the popular knitting patterns which readers would get their mums or grannies to knit.

I was promoted to Fashion Editor and travelled to London on my own, to commission and brief illustrators and shoot covers – and very occasionally a fashion shoot, as most of the time we worked with different illustrators. I was still only 18, and I went on the overnight sleeper (digestive biscuit and a cup of tea in the morning), checked into a hotel, and went everywhere by black taxi to choose clothes at different press offices around the capital.

I loved those trips to London, and would always come home with something new that couldn't be found in Scotland. I bought white skinny jeans from Fiorucci, western boots somewhere on Oxford Street, a boiler suit from Stirling Cooper and vintage lacey tops and petticoats from Antiquarius – a market on Kings Road.

I chose clothes for the pages from Way In at Harrods, Laura Ashley, Miss Selfridge, and Etam to name but a few.

Nina had told me to meet with the illustrators at the best restaurants

Nina Myskow

and cafés – the Fountain Restaurant, at Fortnum and Mason, afternoon tea at The Waldorf Hotel, or cream cakes at Richoux in Kensington. This country bumpkin tried to masquerade as a girl about town . . . but it was hard not to be over-awed.

I'm still proud of my first fashion shoot which featured two girls dressed in Fair Isle jumpers, dresses, and skirts with petticoats showing, which was photographed in the hairdresser's Molton Brown, on South Molton Street, which had a floral wallpapered salon upstairs.

I had a great time working at "Jackie" and am so thankful that I had such an amazing opportunity and start to my career.

Today, it's lovely to meet up with those fellow "Jackie" staffers and remember the good old days. As for being a "Jackie" cover girl, I'm still dining out on that. It's my claim to fame!

TERRIFIC TARTAN!

This season brings a host of lovely colours and fabrics. Ethnic style blanket ponchos in tapestry patterns, and stripes, as well as super mohair, corduroy, cottons and lots more. By far the favourite fabric is tartan, though, and we think it's fantastic!

Look out for super tartan blanket shawls, zip-up lumber jackets, shirts, ponchos, tabards, and tartan trims and ties on everything!

Most tartans are bold red checks, but there are nice variations on this. We found this great tabard from Made In Heaven. It comes in lovely shades of pinks and greens and has twisted wool ties at the sides.

It's really warm, made in wool, and looks good worn with a polo neck, or cowl neck underneath. It costs £10.00 from Jean Junction, London SW1; selected boutiques and department stores. Enquiries to Made In Heaven, 6 Garrick Street, London WC2 (enclose an s.a.e.).

Jackie

EVERYONE knows that "Jackie" was the greatest magazine in the world, but what you might not know – but may have guessed – was just how much fun it was to work on writing and editing your favourite mag!

When ex-military man Gordon Small realised there was a gap in the market to launch a new magazine exclusively for teenage girls (not just a copy of their mum's publications full of dull short stories), he knew the only folk to produce it were people who could relate directly with the teenagers who would adore this magazine.

So the amazing staff were mostly older teenagers, many having just left school, and the mag was edited by talented women often in their late twenties.

They knew that girls needed "Jackie" magazine to be a sort of big sister, a voice that advised them not as a parent or teacher, but a fun, empathetic, wiser pal. People who knew which pop stars they fancied, the coolest clothes to buy, the beauty tips to get rid of the greasiest hair or spottiest chin, the fun quizzes that would be read out to

your friends and, of course, caring Cathy and Claire to sort out every relationship problem. This was exciting and new – a magazine girls from all over the UK and from every background wanted to read. If you were a teen between 1964 and 1993, "Jackie" was your bible!

The interview for a job on "Jackie" was not so much, "Where do you see yourself in five years time?" as, "Who do you think would be a better cover star, Donny or David Cassidy?"The correct answer was always both, obviously!

The first responsibility any trainee magazine journalist was given was putting together the letters page. That's when we saw what you, the readers, cared about most, ensuring we could to write features we knew you'd be desperate to read every Thursday!

As you can imagine, working in an office with lots of other young people, mainly girls, was laugh a minute! Everyone was creative, bursting with ideas for articles and even new ways to print pin-ups . . .

Three-part George Michael door poster, anyone? Roles were usually allocated based on your interests, so if you loved clothes, you had the opportunity to work on the fashion pages, if you enjoyed reading, the photo stories were maybe the best fit for you . . . and if you were a music fan, you could end up interviewing Duran Duran. Simply, the best job ever!

There was dancing around to the freebie albums on the office record player and fabulous beauty draws where your name was called from a hat and you were allowed to take a new product from the heaving beauty samples sent in by companies all trying to have their make-up, shampoo or skincare featured in "Jackie"!

The office phone would ring and it would be Adam Ant calling for his interview with the Pop Ed, but she'd have to make it quick as there was an office outing to see "ET" at the cinema that evening! True story!

So many amazing memories of being part of the biggest teen magazine – here are just some of them from the people privileged enough to bring you your beloved "Jackie" every single week . . .

Jackie Brown

Secrets of life at Jackie

■ Most of the staff were young women, but the young guys on "Jackie" often turned out to be among the best writers and the funniest team members. They all had one thing in common – they were happy to discuss the most girly of subjects during brainstorming sessions.

■ Press officers would send in beauty samples and records for review purposes. Many of those records were sold on to provide extra income in Dundee's second-hand record stores, Groucho's and Rockpile!

■ Pop stars used to drop in to the "Jackie" offices for interviews if they were touring in the area. Steve Strange of Visage, Bronski Beat and Bananarama all stalked the famous DC Thomson third floor. It took a lot to impress, though.

■ The team had a whopping 90-minute lunch hour. And it wasn't unusual to go out for lunch – and a few drinks. Some afternoons, not much work was done!

■ As well as "Jackie", the third floor of DC Thomson's Dundee HQ was home to "Blue Jeans" and "Patches" magazines. There was plenty of rivalry between the teams – but lots of friendships, too. At Christmas, the third floor turned into one big party palace, as wine flowed (in mugs, so the bosses didn't realise!) and all three teams enjoyed chat and japes together.

■ "I remember Strawberry Switchblade coming in once. Unfortunately it was a Friday at 5pm and everyone was heading out to the pub and that took priority for most of us – there was a mass exodus of excited staff members heading down the stairs, while the Strawberry Switchblade girls were battling their way up!" remembers one staff member.

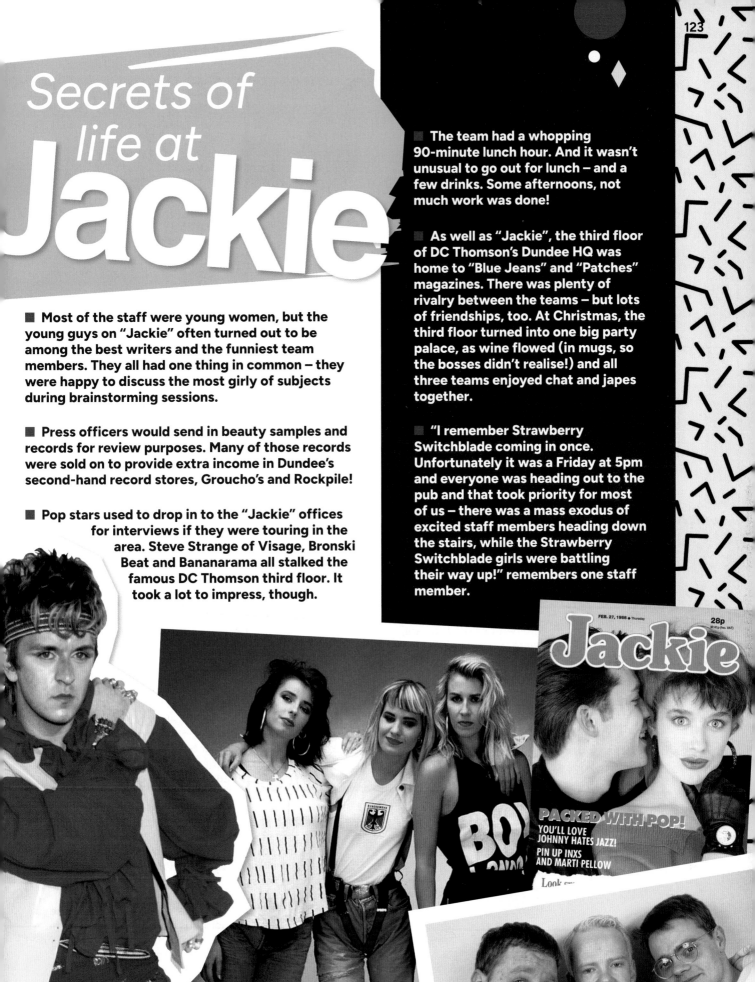

FEB. 27, 1988 ◆ Thursday 28p
(6.41p inc. VAT)

Jackie

PACKED WITH POP!
YOU'LL LOVE JOHNNY HATES JAZZ!
PIN UP INXS AND MARTI PELLOW

Look

It's almost like a job on "Jackie" was written in the stars for Fiona Gibson! She's now a best-selling author, but way back in the early 80s she had a definite DC Thomson dream! It started on a fab little comic called "TV Tops"...

Fiona

Memories Of A
Jac

AS a teenager I'd been drawing cartoons and sending them off to DC Thomson in Dundee – they were published in a comic called "TV Tops" and I was paid a fiver a pop. I'd also written in, asking about jobs on "Jackie" – but advised by the very kind Managing Editor, Gordon Small, to apply again after my Highers (like A-Levels in Scotland). But the world of magazines seemed like an impossible, glamorous dream.

I really didn't know what to do after school. I was set on being an illustrator, but I'd applied to Glasgow School of Art and not got in, and was devastated. It didn't feel like university was for me. Then I was invited to come in for an interview as DC Thomson were taking on a bunch of new recruits for their magazines in Dundee. In a fizzle of nerves I turned up in a sparkly jumper from What Every Woman Wants – like a forerunner to Primark – plus rust coloured cords, hoping to impress!

I was interviewed by Maggie Dun, then Editor of "Jackie", and offered a job. But

not on "Jackie" – new recruits were put in the Central Fiction department, a kind of holding tank for newbies where we'd read the short stories that poured in, literally hundreds every week. We had to sort them into piles of "yes", "shows promise" and "definitely no". A few weeks on, Maggie plucked me out of Central Fiction and said she wanted me for "Jackie".

I was a junior writer at first, writing a column called Weekspot ("something fun or silly to do every day of the week") and the horoscopes, which I knew nothing about – I didn't even know the star signs. I just made them up, quite happily, and wrote any other bits and bobs required of me.

Immediately, the "Jackie" office felt like home. I adored it. Apart from Maggie, her deputy Fiona and typist May – plus the layout guys – the editorial team all sat round a huge messy desk. Records played, chatter flowed and there was much laughter and dancing. We'd throw ideas around and pop star interviews would be conducted from the phone in the little booth at the end of the office.

The office was basically a big bunch of mates, mostly teenagers ourselves – I was 17 when I started. My first day there, it was Maggie's birthday and we all went out en masse and stayed out all night, partying in pubs and winding up dancing on the beach and heading to Maggie's house in Broughty Ferry for breakfast. Then we all tumbled off to the office, to start a day's work, as if nothing unusual had happened. I couldn't believe my luck at being part of it all.

I wrote features and then moved over into fashion. Our fashion pages had been illustrated – those gorgeous drawings everyone remembers and loves. But in the early 80s, photography seemed more contemporary, and I started travelling to London for one week a month, on the sleeper train usually, to put together a month's worth of shoots.

I'd book the photographers, models, hair and make-up people and gather enormous quantities of clothes from fashion PRs. I was 19 at this point, staying in a hotel just off Oxford Street, or the then-sleazy Strand Palace.

Our regular photographers and models became friends. Occasionally, they'd come up to Dundee and we'd do some photo shoots there. One time, a photographer James and his model girlfriend stayed in my filthy houseshare where mushrooms sprouted from the bathroom carpet.

I'd had a load of clothes sent up from London and needed to return them to the fashion PRs. Every night, a

kie Girl

Cathy

Cathy Cassidy is now a best-selling children's author and her love of words started in 1984 when Dundee . . . and a job on "Jackie" magazine beckoned!

I STARTED work on "Jackie" mag in January 1984 – I moved up from Liverpool with my boyfriend Liam and our cat Hamish. I'd just graduated from art school, dressed in 1950s vintage and with a head full of dreams and ideas. That first morning we had a meeting to plan a spring special. In at the deep end! I managed to pitch some ideas, but really I was office junior – I spent a lot of time at the photocopier and answering the phone, both of which were slightly terrifying! I'd dreamed of working on "Jackie" ever since my early teens – the mag had been my bible for years and I'd bombarded it with endless badly typed short stories. Most came back with a polite rejection, but a few got encouraging feedback, and when I was 16 a different teen mag published and paid for my first short story.

Now, I was sitting right next to the Fiction Ed's desk, where piles of short stories towered skywards. Occasionally they'd wobble and manuscripts would fall onto my desk, and the Fiction Ed would ask me to read and comment on them. Some I'd suggest we politely reject, some I loved and hoped we'd publish. My comments must have been OK, because a few weeks later a new office junior appeared, I was given the job of Fiction Ed and the existing Fiction Ed became Assistant Ed. I got to edit stories, suggest series, commission illustrators and nurture new writers and artists . . . cool! I even got to abridge and serialise my favourite 80s movie, "Pretty In Pink"!

The "Jackie" office was a crazy, creative and sometimes chaotic place where young people exchanged awesome ideas and then made them happen. It was old fashioned and untidy with only two ancient sit-up-and-beg typewriters between 12 or so editorial staff, but it was loads of fun and never, ever dull. You never knew who might wander through the office, from Strawberry Switchblade to Erasure and many more! I helped the Fashion Ed on several shoots, and I got to set up a few shoots of my own. My favourite model was Shirley Manson, later lead singer of the band Garbage, who let me dress her in tattered velvet and perch fake birds in her hair. Sometimes we'd be sent on the sleeper train to London to work with London models and photographers, borrowing the latest clothes from the coolest shops! Once I was sent on a ski trip with assorted "real" journalists . . . they did a double take when I turned up for my first lesson wearing a Flip cotton anorak, sticky-out skirt and leggings. Oops!

I got married while working on "Jackie" and everyone from the office came. Soon after I left to teach, freelance and raise a family, moving to rural south-west Scotland, and when "Jackie" finally folded, I became the agony aunt of "Shout", the tween mag that replaced it. I kept in touch with many pals from those times and have such happy memories of those days. There really was so much talent and creativity in that chaotic little office – and for a while, we really did have the best job in the world!

Cathy Cassidy, children's author

lorry went to and from Dundee to our (tiny) office in Fleet Street (the main operation was in Dundee). I hauled a huge bin liner of clothes to the office, ready to go on the London bound lorry. In the "Jackie" office, I opened the bag just to check all was in order.

It wasn't. Instead of clothes, I'd lugged a bin liner of my houseshare's domestic waste into the office. Can, bottles, eggshells – somehow I'd thought it was a sack of clothes! I screamed and ran home, and rescued the bin liner of clothes that had been put out for the bin men.

Many of us shared flats as well as working on "Jackie" together. My friend Jane and I shared the mushroom carpet house, as well as working on "Jackie" and holidaying together. We were virtually the same person!

Every evening at 5pm we'd all surge into the office loos to slap on our make-up ready for a night of pubbing and perhaps clubbing later, in one of Dundee's few hotspots.

I had the best time of my life. It literally set my path for life as 40 years on, I'm still obsessed with magazines and writing, and now write romantic comedy novels for a living. Many of the team are still friends. Things would have turned out very differently if I'd got into Glasgow School of Art.

Fiona Gibson, best-selling novelist

Tracey

Perm-tastic 80s!

BACK in October 1987 a young lassie with wide eyes and a bad perm walked through the very impressive doors of DC Thomson ready to embark on a journey that she would never forget. I was excited and terrified! This was the home of not only "Jackie", but "Blue Jeans", "Patches" and "The Beano"!

The "Jackie" office was buzzing and EVERYONE seemed so cool and confident. It was amazing. The Pop Ed was blasé about interviewing stars and waltzing off to London all the time and here I was, straight out of school, the new office junior!

You learned on the job. You got to do a bit of everything and I couldn't believe that as well as photo-copying, opening mail and never having to buy records or make-up again . . . I got to write the horoscopes! That's correct . . . they were completely made up!

It really was a magical time and it suddenly became the norm to be interviewing pop, film and TV stars, working on the photo stories and going on regular trips to London.

Life on the third floor was one big party . . . you always got your copy in though! Three teenage magazines meant that the place was full of people your age who couldn't wait for nights out. I still have so many great friends who I first met on that floor.

Pop stars would come up to Dundee as part of their press obligations and I can remember a very boozy lunch with Aswad . . . they were so lovely and really wanted to join the "Beano" fan club! After that lunch we all trooped back to the "Beano" office – much to the surprise of the lads in there – and they were formally enrolled!

Tracey Steel, "Jackie" staff member

EVEN now, more than 30 years since the final issue, "Jackie" magazine holds a special, soft, squidgy spot in the hearts of ex-readers and ex-staffers alike. The old girl's become a bit of a national treasure - and fair do's, she deserves it

I was lucky enough to work on the magazine throughout the 80s. I started off as office junior, spent some time on the problems pages (I was both Cathy AND Claire!), moved on to be Pop Editor and then finally "Jackie" Editor. Being Pop Editor was the dream gig. I have stories that I've been dining out on – breakfast, lunch and pre-theatre dinner – for years. Like partying with George Michael and discussing scented candles with Whitney Houston. I'm currently writing a book about my memories of that time.

"Jackie" was a combination of best friend and big sister to the majority of Britain's teenage girls. Readers trusted us. We didn't patronise them. How could we? We were just a keen but green raggedy band of young people, away from home for the first time. Often from small, rural towns just like them, and not much older or more worldly-wise than they were. The office was like an eternal sleepover party. We shared flats and fashion tips and big bags of Flumps. We'd helped each other surreptitiously search for missing copy or transparencies on desks untidier than any teenager's bedroom. We danced round the desks to the radio on Friday afternoons. We all grew up together.

Gayle Anderson, former "Jackie" Editor

Gayle

THIS IS AWFUL. I'M BEING SO SELFISH. I SHOULD BE GRATEFUL FOR MY PRESENTS . . . BUT I CAN'T HELP THINKING ABOUT WHAT THE FORTUNE TELLER SAID.

I JOINED "Jackie" in the mid-80s. I was 18 and I'd previously written horoscopes for a romantic story magazine and then been the fiction editor for another teen weekly in the DC Thomson stable, "Patches".

When the Editor of "Patches", Maggie Dun, moved next door to the top job on "Jackie" she took me with her. Heaven knows why! I was lazy but had good hair. And "Jackie" was the big leagues.

It was like being at school which was just as well since most of us were in our first jobs out of education. We wrote our articles on very shiny notepads and then gave them to the office typist – you read that right – who typed them up. One day I managed to find a heavy old typewriter and decided I would teach myself how to use it. My plodding one-finger technique is the one I still proudly use today!

We would have parties in the office at Christmas time and on Royal Wedding days. Maggie was a staunch monarchist. One time we all brought party food in. The jelly I made was hideous and didn't set so it stayed in a Tupperware box under my desk for months. Chances are it's still there now.

I interviewed pop stars, got lots of free records and gig tickets and even had my own infrequent column where, as Our Mike, I wrote about relationships. It was an absolutely dream job.

On one famous occasion I hosted my own double page photo story in the "Jackie" Annual 1986 which we shot in the "Jackie" offices. And I also appeared as Mr December alongside Morten Harket from A-ha and Wham's George Michael on the "Jackie" multiple-part pull-out-and-keep calendar.

My stay on "Jackie" lasted about 18 months and the end came by accident. On a trip as the Pop Editor down to London from the editorial offices in Dundee, I was offered a job on the spot during a meeting with the head of Virgin Records' press office. The salary was five times more than my earnings in Dundee and the job came with a car.

I really never meant to leave "Jackie", but it was a good end to a very happy period of my career.

Mike Soutar, Entreprenuer and star of "The Apprentice"

DC Thomson's Dundee Meadowside building

Mike

Hello!

Lucy

Memories Of A Jac

THE year was 1987, hair was BIG, shoulder-pads were bigger, and eyeliner was bright blue.

That's when I joined DC Thomson, publisher of "Jackie" magazine. And although our official address was 185 Fleet Street, the Dundee office was home to the "Jackie" office!

THE JACKIE OFFICE

In the 1980s, the whole of the third floor was given over to the teen mags, with "Blue Jeans" and "Patches" just along the corridor from "Jackie".

Most of us on the floor were in our early 20s at most. Lots of us shared flats, and there were regular nights out, which often began around half past four with hair and make-up being done in the (wood-panelled) ladies powder room.

With Radio 1 always on in the background, we had two phones for the whole office – one of which was in a booth to allow for celebrity interviews.

Without computers, our massive wooden (splintery) desks were covered in work on the go, pages to be read, and freebies from PRs. And in the days before health and safety, smoking was still allowed – with all that paper around!

HOROSCOPES

The office junior's main jobs were going to the canteen and writing the horoscopes.

It was all in good fun, and if it was vague, it was fine. Libras! You MAY meet a handsome stranger! Leos! Your luck COULD be about to change!

All written on paper known as 'bumf' (which gives you an indication of its quality).

TEENSCOPE
for week beginning October 30.

LIBRA (Sept. 22-Oct. 22)
No matter how difficult it seems, you're going to have to curb that hasty temper of yours or you'll end up in a lot of trouble.

SCORPIO (Oct. 23-Nov. 21)
That effort you made a few weeks ago will pay off—perhaps even with a cash bonus. A party you go to rather reluctantly will turn out to be a great success.

SAGITTARIUS (Nov. 22-Dec. 21)
Keep an eye on that boy—he could be thinking of making a move. Just because your friend goes on a spending spree doesn't mean you have to go on one, too.

CAPRICORN (Dec. 22-Jan. 19)
Your natural shyness could cause one or two problems when you go somewhere new, but once you make one friend you'll find yourself making more and more.

AQUARIUS (Jan. 20-Feb. 18)
Call on a friend you've not seen for a while—your visit will be appreciated. Have some early nights this you're going to need al get through the week

PISCES (Feb.
You could Thursday, bu something imp You'll catch the

ARIES (Mar.
Money matters midweek, when yo unexpected expense. M relax and enjoy yourself on Friday

TAURUS (Apr. 21-May 20)

TECHNOLOGY -FREE ZONE

No mobile phones or email meant everything ran more slowly.

We had a long lead time – the time between everything being written and it going on sale. It was around twelve weeks, so everything had to be written ahead of time.

80'S

kie Girl

WOW!

THE PROBLEM PAGE

I had different roles while working on the magazine. First up, I dealt with the problem page, which was then called "Dear Ellie".

This involved working with the real Ellie, who answered the questions which appeared on the page, and then I took over handling the responses.

Some problems were serious, but most were about looks, feelings, and boys – how to let someone know you like them, how to let someone down gently, what to do if he doesn't know you exist.

Lots of letters were to do with growing up – not being comfortable in your own skin, not liking the way you look.

Family issues featured quite a lot – not getting on with siblings, parents getting divorced.

Body problems were common, too – periods, spots and sweating were all popular.

Every problem sent in with a stamped addressed envelope was answered.

I also worked on what had to be one of the most popular "Jackie" features – the photo stories!

PHOTO STORIES

We had two or three of these a week, and it was lots of fun – and lots of work, with multiple stories in different stages of production on the go at any one time.

Stories came in firstly written out frame-by-frame. These were read in the usual way and approved before being sent out to a photographer.

The photographers we used had their own models and took pics to match each frame, being careful to leave space for the speech bubbles which our artists would add later.

When it all came into the office, we then cut out the best pic for each frame, then stuck them all down in order, with Cow Gum and a spatula. High-tech – not!

FAMOUS FACES

Lots of us on the floor appeared in photo stories. And famous faces who appeared include Alan Cumming, Fiona Bruce, and Mike Soutar from "The Apprentice" .

Wouldn't it be great to get them back for an up-to-date photo story!

THE THIRD FLOOR

It's funny in the age of hybrid and home working, to look back on what it was like in those days. It was so busy, and people were constantly coming and going – between the magazines, or onto other jobs or Uni.

People working hard but also playing cricket in the corridors, dyeing their hair at their desks (!) and sleeping off hangovers in the stationery cupboard.

Make-overs were popular – where readers would have hair and make-up done, try out the latest styles and have it all photographed for the magazine. Above is a pic from one I was in!

Prior to the shoots, we'd stick tape on the bottom of the shoes, which were borrowed from shops in Dundee.

I think we knew by the 80s that the heyday of "Jackie" had passed, but I then went on to work on the mysteriously-named "Project B", later known as "Shout", which entertained readers for nearly 30 years before ceasing publication in 2023.

Happy days!